DATE DUE

NOV 1 2 97	JAN 0 2 2001	
JUN 1 0 98		
NOV 2 0 1993	MAR 2 6 2001	
MAR 0 2 '94		
MAY 1 4 1994	MAY 1 5 2002	
OCT 1 0 1994	OCT 0 5 2004	
	NOV 2 9 2004	
DEC 1 2 1995	MAY 9 2 2006	
MAR 2 5 1996		
APR 2 2 1996		
OCT 2 8 1996 1997		
1 2 NOV 1997		

Mechanicsburg Public Library

Mechanicsburg, Ohio 43044

1. Books may be kept two weeks and may be renewed once for the same period, except 7 day books and magazines.

2. A fine is charged for each day a book is not returned according to the above rule. No book will be issued to any person incurring such a fine until it has been paid.

3. All injuries to books beyond reasonable wear and all losses shall be made good to the satisfaction of the Librarian.

4. Each borrower is held responsible for all books charged on his card and for all fines accruing on the same.

DEMCO

HISTORY OF THE WORLD

Europe at the Time of Greece and Rome

RAINTREE PUBLISHERS
Milwaukee

This book has been reviewed for accuracy by
Prof. Frank N. Egerton, Dept. of History,
University of Wisconsin-Parkside, Kenosha, Wisconsin.

History of the World by Editoriale Jaca Book s.p.a., Milano. Copyright © 1985
by Editoriale Jaca Book.

English translation copyright © 1989 Raintree Publishers Limited Partnership.
Published in the United States by Raintree Publishers.

Translated by Hess-Inglin Translation Service.

1 2 3 4 5 6 7 8 9   93 92 91 90 89

Library of Congress Number: 88-24003

Printed and bound in the United States of America.

Library of Congress Cataloging-in-Publication Data

Europa ai tempi di Grecia e Roma. English.
   Europe at the time of Greece and Rome.

   (History of the World)
   Translation of: L'Europa ai tempi di Grecia e Roma.
   Includes index.
   1. Europe—History—To 476. I. Title. II. Series.
 D80.E9513   1988   936—dc19   88-24003
 ISBN 0-8172-3305-9

Cover illustration by Francis Balistreri.

TABLE OF CONTENTS

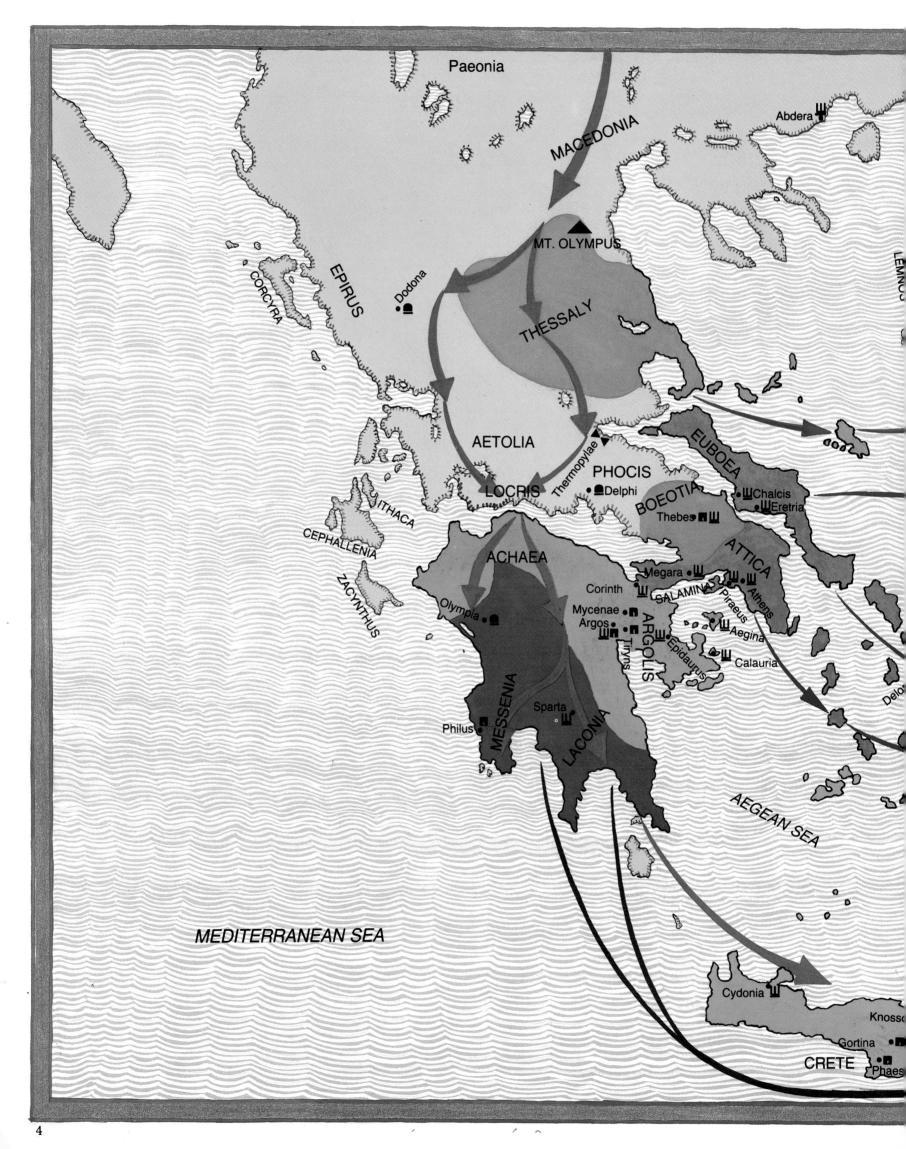

Paeonia

MACEDONIA

Abdera

MT. OLYMPUS

EPIRUS

CORCYRA

Dodona

THESSALY

AETOLIA

Thermopylae

LOCRIS

PHOCIS

Delphi

EUBOEA

Chalcis

Eretria

BOEOTIA

Thebes

ATTICA

ITHACA

CEPHALLENIA

ACHAEA

Megara

Corinth

SALAMIS

Athens

Piraeus

ZACYNTHUS

Olympia

Mycenae

Argos

ARGOLIS

Aegina

Tiryns

Epidaurus

Calauria

MESSENIA

Sparta

Philus

LACONIA

AEGEAN SEA

MEDITERRANEAN SEA

LEMNOS

Delos

Cydonia

Knossos

Gortina

CRETE

Phaestos

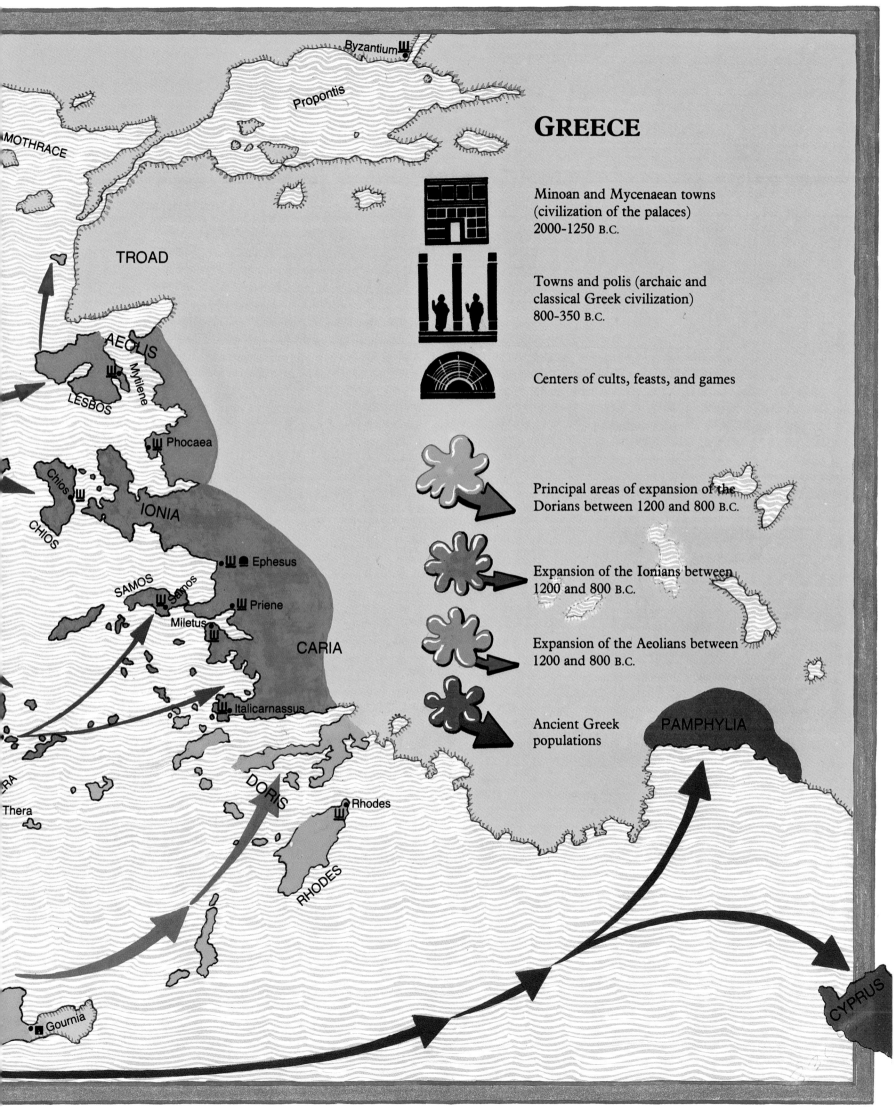

GREECE

Minoan and Mycenaean towns
(civilization of the palaces)
2000-1250 B.C.

Towns and polis (archaic and
classical Greek civilization)
800-350 B.C.

Centers of cults, feasts, and games

Principal areas of expansion of the
Dorians between 1200 and 800 B.C.

Expansion of the Ionians between
1200 and 800 B.C.

Expansion of the Aeolians between
1200 and 800 B.C.

Ancient Greek
populations

Byzantium

Propontis

MOTHRACE

TROAD

AEOLIS

Mytilene

LESBOS

Phocaea

Chios

CHIOS

IONIA

Ephesus

SAMOS

Samos

Priene

Miletus

CARIA

Italicarnassus

DORIS

Rhodes

RHODES

PAMPHYLIA

Thera

Gournia

CYPRUS

THE GREEK CIVILIZATION

In the eighth century B.C., one of the fundamental pages of human history was about to open. The group of islands and peninsulas which today is known as Greece was to be the stage for extraordinary events.

Highly developed civilizations had flourished in the past both in Greece and on the large island of Crete. The Greek towns of Mycenae and Tiryns, flourished and hosted a great blossoming of the arts around 1400-1200 B.C. This period is called the Mycenaean period. It was followed by the so-called Dark Ages between 1200 and 800 B.C. Mycenaean civilization, which was ruled by powerful lords who lived in large palaces, was destroyed by drought, raids, and a progressive decay of the Greek towns. During this time of darkness, the previous period began to be looked on as a heroic and mythical age.

Politics

The art of politics was born in Greece. The polis or city-state was a genuine Greek achievement. Noble citizens, at first, and then an increasingly large number of ordinary citizens were involved in politics. The Greek people conceived a system of written laws, which stated the rights of the powerful as well as those of any other citizen. Everyone had to obey the written laws. This system of laws was proof of the political intellect of the Greek people. They did not trust the judgement of a sovereign (a supreme ruler) and his power to decide what was right and wrong. In difficult times or because of internal clashes, the Greeks would often resort to putting the rule of the polis in the hands of tyrants. In spite of this, their love for the law was never obscured.

Philosophy

A major philosophical movement originated in Greece. At its core was the importance of reason, considered the ultimate characteristic of humans. Greek rationality was to become a reference point for all western civilization. However, Greek thought was often tainted with pessimism. Often, humans were considered incapable of finding the answers to the deepest questions and of understanding death.

Art

A great appreciation for the beauty, intelligence, and strength of humans developed in Greece. Greek art depicted the beauty of human beings as never before.

THE GREEKS INVENT THE POLIS

After 800 B.C., a period of three hundred years known as the Archaic Age started in Greece. This period was followed by the Classical Age. At the beginning of the Archaic Age, numerous villages were scattered throughout the Greek territory. Some were of ancient origin; others had been created by newly settled populations. A king was the head of each village. He was no more than a tribal leader, the head of the most important family in the village. He was not an absolute sovereign and did not hold all power in his hands. The principal members of other powerful families, the nobles, also shared in the power. Gradually, the importance of the monarchs decreased, and the nobles became the rulers of the growing villages. This form of power was called oligarchy. Besides increasing in size and population, many villages began to establish relationships with each other. Thus, new units of territory originated formed by several villages and by the surrounding countryside. These groups of villages, whose territory was often extensively farmed, were the first step toward the creation of the well-known polis. The polis was not a single town; several villages could be included within its territory, and one of them would become the dominant village. The main feature of the polis was that all the people living within its territory felt that they belonged to the same unit, not only a territorial unit, but a political unit as well.

It is not by chance that the word *politics* is derived from the word *polis*. An acropolis was built in the polis, usually on an elevated location. On the acropolis, temples were erected, creating an important place for all citizens.

Not far from the acropolis, a meeting area was created called the agora. It consisted of a square with houses around it. The agora formed the heart of the polis, becoming the center for economic exchange. What makes it important in history is the fact that it was the chosen place for political life. In the beginning, the agora was the meeting point for the heads of families. The members of the oligarchy would gather there to make decisions concerning the government of the polis. These members were landowners, very wealthy farmers who had servants. Peasants and traders who eventually acquired some wealth were also allowed to participate in political life. In order to take part in political decisions, it was necessary to be a citizen. This privilege extended to all the people who were native of the territory of the polis. Foreigners who moved to a particular polis could never become citizens. Women were citizens but did not participate in political acts.

The Greeks invented a new form of political and social structure, the polis. It was formed by the unification of city and countryside. Shown is the acropolis, the heart of this unification.

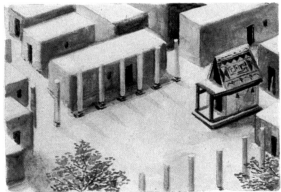

The agora was the meeting point for the population of the polis and was used as a market and assembly area. It was also a religious area with temples and altars.

Depicted is the ancient agora of Calauria.

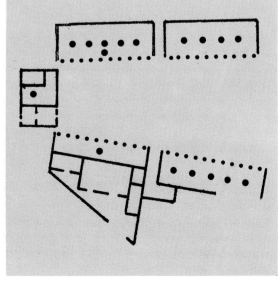

Nation and Homeland

In order to understand what a Greek state was, imagine a stretch of territory with a large valley, forested slopes, bottom pastures, fields, vineyards, and olive groves vast enough to sustain ten thousand people. The territory also included a mountain or hill, which could be used as a shelter in case of attack, and a harbor for trade with neighboring states. At times, the town was surrounded by defensive walls.

The essence of a polis was based on the passion that the citizens of the city-states felt about their independence. The city-states were independent entities with their own laws, currency, systems of weights and measure, and sacred territorial marker stones.

Most important of all, they had faith in their protector gods and goddesses, in their ancestors, and in a primal father. All of these concepts formed the identity of the country.

1. Eretria
2. Ephesus
3. Rhodes
4. Corinth
5. Chalcis

25
33
37
26
38
35
31
18
32
11 12
20
15
13
19
30
14 17
16 24
39

11. Metapontion
12. Tarentum
13. Croton
14. Agrigentum
15. Sybaris

THE EXPANSION OF GREECE: HELLAS

In the early 700s B.C., Greece began to expand and establish settlements along the coasts of the Aegean Sea, the Black Sea, and the central and western Mediterranean Sea. For two hundred years, the Greek world grew constantly larger. It eventually clashed with Phoenicians and later with Carthaginians, who gained dominion over sea traffic.

The Colonization Movement

Varied reasons prompted the beginning of Greek colonization: population growth, political oppression, social malaise, the need to conquer new markets and new territories, and the drive for heroic adventure. In the beginning, colonization was carried on by groups of farmers. Later it became controlled by the city-states. A colony was politically independent and

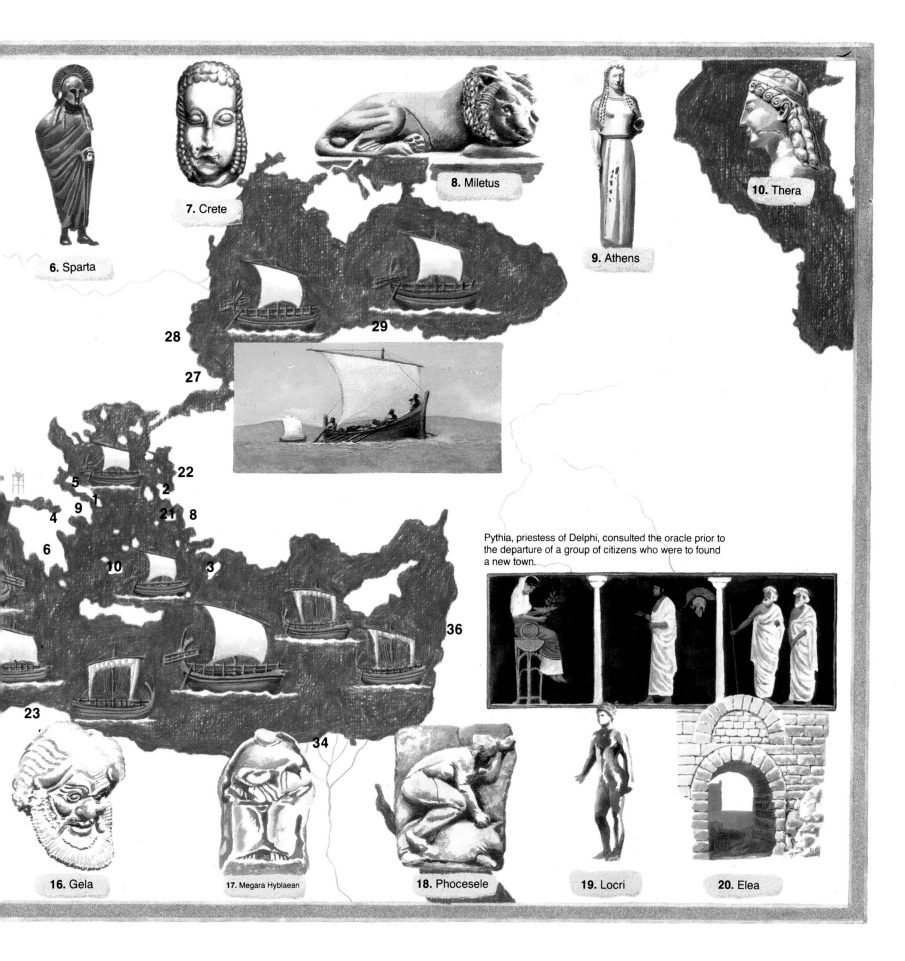

6. Sparta

7. Crete

8. Miletus

9. Athens

10. Thera

28

29

27

22

5
2
1
9
21
8
4
6
10
3
36
23
34

Pythia, priestess of Delphi, consulted the oracle prior to the departure of a group of citizens who were to found a new town.

16. Gela

17. Megara Hyblaean

18. Phocesele

19. Locri

20. Elea

had its own laws.

Hellas

Mother towns and colonies together did not form an empire, which is to say they did not have a common government. In spite of this, the colonization process made the towns even stronger. The group of poleis which gradually developed in the Greek territory together with the colonies in other territories is called Hellas. The Greek people would maintain their language and religion in the colonies and retain strong commercial and cultural relationships with Greece. The Greek language had developed in ancient times and because of colonization, spread throughout the shores of the Mediterranean. Soon it became the prominent language in many towns. Also, the religious bonds between the colonies and Greece were strongly felt.

OLIGARCHY

FARMERS, MERCHANTS, ARTISANS

FOREIGNERS (metics)

POOR FARMERS
People who did not always have enough land to sustain themselves and their families

FOREIGNERS (metics)

THETES
People with no personal possessions who lived precariously or were at the service of wealthy families

SERVANTS
The offspring of subjugated people, poor citizens enslaved because of debts, or foreign people who had been defeated and enslaved

The structure of Greek society

The Birth of Currency

Starting in the seventh century B.C., currency began to be used for commercial trade in the Mediterranean region. Previous to the introduction of currency, barter was the means of trade. The kingdoms of Asia Minor were the first to use coins, soon followed by the Greek polis. Coins were made of precious metals (gold, silver, or bronze), had a determined weight, and were marked with the symbol of the king or of the town where they were struck. The value of the coins was based upon the trust which the wealth and power of the issuing country inspired. In a very short time, currency gained enormous importance in the economy. It was accepted by all, both on the market and as compensation for work. It spread rapidly and even reached lands where the power of the issuing country was not felt. It attracted merchants and goods, improved the economic patterns of the issuing country, and extended the influence of that country.

1. *Left:* An electrum, a gold and silver alloy coin with a lion head from Smyrna, 575 B.C. *Right:* A silver coin dedicated to the river god Gela, from Greater Greece, approximately 480 B.C. **2.** A blacksmith and his tools are depicted on an amphora from Attica, end of the sixth century B.C. **3.** Shown is an example of the Archaic alphabet. **4.** This inscription on a stone forms a list of names. It is from Thera, second half of the sixth century B.C.

Technology and the Alphabet

During the Archaic epoch, a great deal of progress was made in technology. The working of iron, which had been developed some centuries earlier, was improved and became widespread. More and more farming and artisan tools as well as weaponry were produced. Plows and better built farming equipment permitted the tillage of impervious areas which could not be farmed before, resulting in an expansion of agriculture. This caused the population explosion which led to colonization. New iron artisan tools and the imitation of Phoenician ships contributed to the improvement in the art of shipbuilding. Ships which could withstand open sea navigation began to be constructed. In cultural life, a major innovation of the period was the introduction of the phonetic alphabet, derived from the Phoenician one. The main feature of this alphabet was that each sound corresponded to a particular character. The Phoenicians used to write only the consonants; the Greeks added the vowels, creating the first complete alphabet.

SOCIAL LIFE IN THE POLIS

From Monarchy to Oligarchy

The king as a figurehead did not completely disappear, but often he would be considered as a superior among equals.

The essence of monarchy no longer existed. A form of government called oligarchy replaced the monarchy. It was formed by the heads of the most important families—landowners, cattle owners, and copper mine owners. In short, they were the representatives of what was at the basis of the economy of the state. This class of aristocrats has been called by various names, but the term which was the most highly regarded was *knights*. It meant that they owned horses which enabled them to go into battle on horseback protected by complex bronze armor. Each of the knights had a shield, a helmet, a cuirass, metal leg covers (greaves), a long lance, and a short sword. The poor farmers, on the other hand, had to fight on foot, and each was equipped with a short javelin.

Changes in Society

Between 700 and 600 B.C., a great economic revolution occurred in Greek society. It was caused by the discovery and colonization of new worlds in the Mediterranean region, the widespread use of currency, iron tools and weapons, and population growth. The owners of fields, pastures, vineyards, and mines, who were used to gaining new wealth by fighting, were now able to use commercial activities to gain riches.

In some towns the landowners remained the dominant class, while elsewhere, especially in the colonies and on the islands, trade activities created a new wealthy class. At times, the offspring of declining families would marry those of rich merchants, thereby narrowing the difference between the old and new aristocracy. Finally, the importance of the middle class was constantly growing. The middle class was composed of farmers, artisans, and merchants and was to achieve an increasingly significant role in the life of the polis.

The Political Institutions of the Polis

The oligarchic society had a different structure in each individual polis. However, it is possible to outline some common political features.

Assembly. The assembly, which had various denominations (ecclesia, alia, apella), was composed of a varying number of individuals forming the so-called group of "active citizens."

Decisions were hardly ever made within the assembly. Most often the assembly would merely approve decisions made by the council or simply give advise on various issues.

Council. The council was a step higher than the assembly. It was a smaller group of people, usually formed by the most wealthy citizens, These were either the most powerful citizens, who had recently acquired wealth, or they were the offspring of the major families in town.

Magistrature. Ruling the polis involved various tasks. At the time of the monarchy, the king was surrounded by a council. Members of the council with special duties were called magistrates, and made up a magistrature. Some magistrates were the heads of the council, such as the ephors in Sparta or the demiurges in various other towns. Others attended to special functions, such as the preservation of customs, the supervision of public works, and the execution of religious ceremonies.

The Tyrants

The birth of the middle class, which among other things allowed for the introduction of the hoplites into the army, caused increasing criticism of the work of the aristocracy.

Greek society was structured into various social classes. The servants were enslaved individuals, followed by the thetes, who were poor peasants. One step higher were the foreigners or metics, both poor and rich, who were constantly trying to gain further rights in the Greek towns. Even though they were never allowed to acquire Greek citizenship, they gradually gained more and more power within the towns. Thus, the polis was a place of contrasts, and the oligarchy had a very hard time trying to rule it due both to internal struggle and to pressure from the middle class. Sometimes, this situation was resolved with the appointment of a new figure, the tyrant. The tyrant was a nobleman who took the ruling of the polis into his hands during particularly hard times and did not have to obey the laws that applied to all the other citizens. Today, the word *tyrant* has a negative connotation, but this did not usually apply to the tyrants of the polis, some of whom were very wise men. The tyrant, who had power over the assembly and the council, was sometimes backed by the lower classes and had the power to modify the law. Some tyrants issued new, just laws and helped in the development of the polis, while others ignored the legislation and ruled in an arbitrary and violent way.

CAVALRYMAN

Changes in the Army: The Hoplites

The military technique was modernized, and new types of warriors called hoplites appeared. Each warrior wore a helmet and a cuirass and carried a round shield, a long lance, and a short sword. Most of the infantry was composed of merchants, artisans, and small landowners who could afford to buy the equipment. They formed the army of the town. Aristocratic chivalry lost much of its importance. Battles pivoted around the clashes of close ranks of warriors who fought in an orderly and unified manner, shoulder to shoulder, protecting each other with their shields. This sense of cohesion and order, of equal rights and reciprocal solidarity, was a basic expression of civil life in the polis and one of the highest priorities of its people.

HOPLITES IN BATTLE

Athens, the largest polis in Attica, was founded on democracy and the right of every adult male citizen to partake in political life. *Inset:* The Athenian government.

ATHENS AND SPARTA

Attica Gathers Around Athens

Attica, a region of Greece which had always been ruled by populations of Ionian descent, was unified under the hegemony of Athens and became a large, united city-state. Attica was a vast, principally agricultural region, ruled by a powerful group of aristocratic landowners. When the power of the kings declined, Athens was ruled by the aristocracy, with a social structure in which the difference between nobles and the lower class was clearly marked.

Increase in Economic Problems

The economic situation in Athens was becoming increasingly difficult, and around the end of the seventh century B.C., dissatisfaction was common among the people of Attica. As a result of the diversification of cultures, the nobles who owned most of the land (grain farms) had to face new economic competition. Some of the wealth-ier farmers had begun to cultivate vineyards, fruit trees, olive trees, and trees for lumber. In addition, they successfully traded their produce. The poor farmers, on the other hand, were continually forced to borrow money in order to survive. Thus, a long chain of debt accumulated through the course of the years, forcing many farmers to lose their land to rich creditors.

The Tyrant of Athens

The social disorders caused by these problems were solved by the noble Pisistratus, who ruled as a tyrant without resorting to violence. He established the basis for further reforms which proved satisfactory to the majority of people in Athens. During his government, Pisistratus also succeeded in extending the hegemony of Athens over the island of Salamis, over some islands of the Aegean Sea, and along the shores of the Hellespont. After his death, his sons Hippias and Hipparchus tried to maintain

THE POLITICAL CONSTITUTION OF ATHENS
The Reform of Solon

Solon decreed a prohibition to loans based on the financial security of people or their land holdings. He did not equally redistribute the land but divided Athenian society into four classes, defined according to the amount of revenue from the owned land. The people belonging to the first two classes formed the cavalry and had access to the main political positions. The magistrates, treasurers, and archons were chosen from this group. The citizens belonging to the third class served in the army as hoplites. There were two organs of democratic control. All male citizens took part in the assembly, and each one had the right to vote. Each male citizen could be part of the heliaea, the tribunal of the people which judged crimes against the

CLASSES OF WEALTH

| PENTAKOSIO-MEDIMNOI 500 modiuses of wheat | KNIGHTS 300 modiuses of wheat | ZEUGITES 200 modiuses of wheat | THETES no proper |

12

The male citizens of Sparta were permitted to train only in war. All of them were involved in constant training through strict discipline and had to share mealtime with war companions.

Inset: The Spartan government

community, even if the accused were members of the noble class.

The Reform of Cleisthenes

The two fundamental objectives of the reform of Cleisthenes were to decrease the power in the hands of the great noble families and to ease the contrasts between the various classes of citizens. He divided Attica into three regions which were geographically and economically different—the mountainous poor area to the north (Diacria), the rich central plain (Pedia), and the coastal area (Paralia), where commercial, artisan, and maritime activities flourished. Each region was divided into districts, each of which was grouped with two others to form a tribe. There was a total of ten tribes. A tribe was the result of a territorial division and was less tightly connected to the family group than ever before. Each tribe had to provide an army of hoplites and elected a strategos as its leader. Each tribe sent fifty representatives to Athens who took part in the council of the five hundred (boule). The ecclesia was regularly summoned to check on the work of the council of the five hundred.

To protect the state against attempts of tyrants to seize power, the reform created the method of ostracism. Citizens had the power to ban from Athens any individual suspected of plotting against the state.

power but Hipparchus was murdered, and Hippias was eventually overthrown with the help of the Spartans. Athens then developed a democratic government under Cleisthenes. Democracy was to be continued in Athens under the leadership of Pericles.

The Dorians Dominate the Achaeans in the Peloponnesus

When the migrating Dorians reached the Peloponnesus, they conquered the eastern region called Laconia and the Achaeans who lived there. The Dorians never blended with the local population. They remained an armed, separate minority.

The Military Democracy of Sparta

The Dorians never ceased to consider themselves an occupation army in Laconia, and this greatly affected their life-style. They had freed themselves from the burden of cultivating the

land but had to be constantly armed and on the defensive. Sparta, the only polis of the region of Laconia, had a barracks-like organization, and its inhabitants were always ready to defend themselves against the enemy, both from the outside and within the town.

The Political Institutions of Sparta

The political structure in Sparta was conceived in order to avoid the possibility of predominance of one individual over all the others. Tyranny was strongly rejected. According to tradition, around 700 B.C., Lycurgus gave Sparta a body of laws to regulate its society. The people of Sparta were supposedly the first among the Greeks to have a complete body of written laws. At the basis of political life was the apella, the assembly of armed men. Most of the power, however, was in the hands of the gerousia, a council formed of twenty-eight gerontes, or elders.

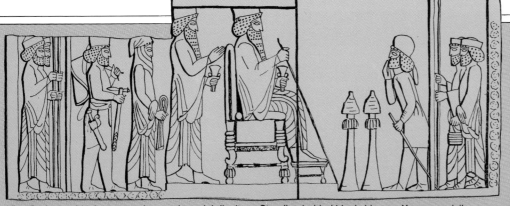

King Darius on his throne receives an imperial dignitary. Standing behind him is his son, Xerxes, a civil servant, and a body guard. This illustration was taken from a bas-relief at Persepolis.

THE PERSIAN WARS

The Persian Empire in Asia Minor

In the mid-sixth B.C., the king of Persia made his state into a great power. He joined the with Greek colonies of Asia Minor. The political system was different from that of the city-states of Greece. The eastern empire was a vast territory inhabited by various populations, all under the guidance of the emperor. The Persian presence in the Aegean Sea facilitated trade activities toward the Orient and was an element of strength from which military and political help could be obtained. The Ionia region, inhabited by Greeks, had become a province of the empire and was governed by tyrants who were faithful to the emperor. In Greece, the outer territories sided with the Persians, while the poleis remained divided on the issue.

Rebellion of the Ionic Towns

In 500 B.C., the tyrant of Miletus rebelled against Persia and installed a democratic government. The rebellion spread to many other Ionic towns, whose inhabitants were also under the economic and political control of the Persians. The Ionians received some help from Athens but were defeated.

At this point, the Persians were interested in Greek territory not only for the wealth which it contained, but also because of the political and military threat which the Greek towns represented, first and foremost Athens. In 490, the Persians destroyed Eretria from the sea and swarmed into the plain of Marathon, about 25 miles (40 kilometers) from Athens. There the hoplites of Athens, lead by Miltiades, though greatly outnumbered, defeated the enemy and forced it to retreat.

The Expedition of Xerxes and the End of the Persian Wars

King Darius's son, Xerxes, succeeded his father in 486 and led expeditions against Greece, both by sea and by land. The Greeks were defeated in the battle of Thermopylae in 480. The Athenian fleet lead by Themistocles met the Persian ships in battle off Salamis, near Athens, and defeated them. The following year, in Plataea, the Greek army defeated the Persian army once and for all.

Democracy: "Free and Equal Citizens"

The freedom of the individual in the Athens of Pericles was very important. A citizen could not be enslaved or made into a servant for any reason. The errors of a citizen could not transfer to his or her family. Every citizen, regardless of riches, was equal before the law. This was the democracy of the people. Each Athenian was a free and equal being. All male citizens could take part in the assembly, where they had the right to speak up and vote. When they were old enough they could become part of the heliaea, the council of the judges. They could be candidates for election to the council and in other magistratures. This was called the sovereignty of the citizens. The citizens could take part in festivities, processions, sacrifices, and games.

The tension caused by the uneven distribution of wealth remained, but Pericles tried to ease it by burdening the wealthy with heavier taxes and protecting the less wealthy. Only the offspring of Athenian people were considered Athenian citizens, but foreigners were coming to Athens in increasing numbers. They were called metics and were allowed to develop trade and economic and artistic activities in an atmosphere of great freedom. It was a common saying that it was better to live in Athens as a metic than in one's own country as a wealthy citizen.

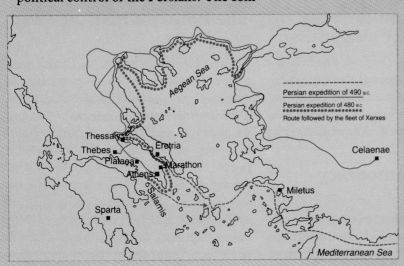

Shown are the routes of the Persian wars. The red broken line indicates the sea route of the first Persian war. The war against Athens was started by Darius in 490 B.C. The Athenians defeated his army in the Battle of Marathon. In 480 an expedition guided by Xerxes attacked the Greek towns, both by land and by sea (solid red line and dotted red line respectively).The expedition of 480 was driven back by the Greeks as a result of their victories at Salamis and Plataea.

Persian expedition of 490 B.C.
Persian expedition of 480 B.C.
Route followed by the fleet of Xerxes

Pictured is Pericles, who ruled Athens during the period of its highest splendor.

In Athens, Pericles is about to enter the Assembly held in the Pnyx, a special amphitheater located on a hill facing the Acropolis.

THE AGE OF PERICLES

The Figure of Pericles

Pericles, born of a wealthy aristocratic Athenian family, supported the democratic party. Under his rule, Athens flourished and became an artistic, cultural, and political center which was admired by all the Greek world.

The Foreign Policy of Athens

Pericles guided his army in various wars. As a result, Athens became a true empire. The Athenians imposed general regulations concerning the administration of the various towns and the type of currency. At times they would send investigators to keep the most rebellious towns under control. The economic control of Athens is evident in the use of currency. The Athenian coins, the famous "owls of Athens" (tetradrachms), were the only currency used in trade between the towns. The Mediterranean became a vast market at the disposal of the Greeks. However, her allies could not obtain political positions in Athens, which was still ruled like a city-state. Only the offspring of Athenian parents were citizens of Athens.

The Splendor of Athens

Athens had an aggressive foreign policy, but its internal policy was highly democratic. Everything was conceived so that the highest possible number of citizens could partake in the political life of the town. A lottery method was applied for choosing most of the men who served in the magistratures. Men who held public positions were paid.

Great commercial wealth accumulated because of the proceeds Athens collected from its empire. Pericles decided that such abundance should be used to remedy the damage caused by the Persians, and started major public works projects. Soon the Acropolis, the agora, and the road leading to the harbor were rebuilt. Athens became the main cultural center of Greece. It was a meeting point for famous artists, writers, and philosophers.

The War of the Peloponnese and the Crisis of the Polis

After the death of Pericles, Athens continued its expansionary policy and, in 415 B.C., organized an expedition to Sicily, which was to end in defeat. The Peloponnesian War between the Athenian empire and the Peloponnesian League under Spartan leadership began in 431 B.C. and ended in 404 B.C. with a victory by the Spartans. They forced Athens to drastically reduce the size of its fleet, to give up all of its territories except for Attica and Salamis, and to destroy the fortifications of the Piraeus Harbor. The Spartan army occupied Athens and supported the violent rule of the Thirty Tyrants. The tyrants harshly persecuted the proponents of democracy. The end of democracy in Athens was a sign of a widespread crisis throughout Greece. The poleis were no longer able to coexist peacefully, and disagreement between them made them weak and unstable.

This silver coin is the well-known "owl of Athens." The owl was the symbol of commerce, and the olive leaves indicated the main agricultural product of the city-state.

The bow of a war ship is depicted on this coin from Sicily.

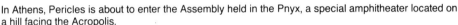

15

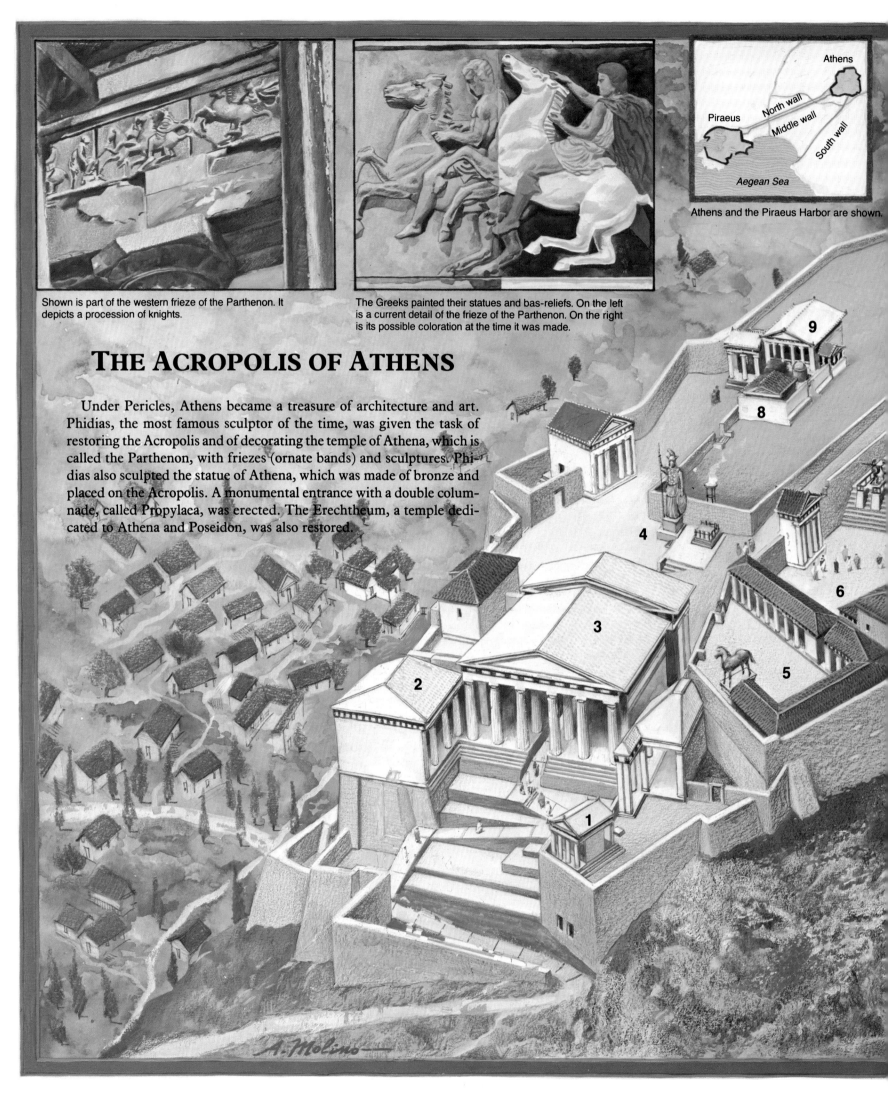

Shown is part of the western frieze of the Parthenon. It depicts a procession of knights.

The Greeks painted their statues and bas-reliefs. On the left is a current detail of the frieze of the Parthenon. On the right is its possible coloration at the time it was made.

Athens and the Piraeus Harbor are shown.

Piraeus
North wall
Middle wall
South wall
Athens
Aegean Sea

THE ACROPOLIS OF ATHENS

Under Pericles, Athens became a treasure of architecture and art. Phidias, the most famous sculptor of the time, was given the task of restoring the Acropolis and of decorating the temple of Athena, which is called the Parthenon, with friezes (ornate bands) and sculptures. Phidias also sculpted the statue of Athena, which was made of bronze and placed on the Acropolis. A monumental entrance with a double columnade, called Propylaea, was erected. The Erechtheum, a temple dedicated to Athena and Poseidon, was also restored.

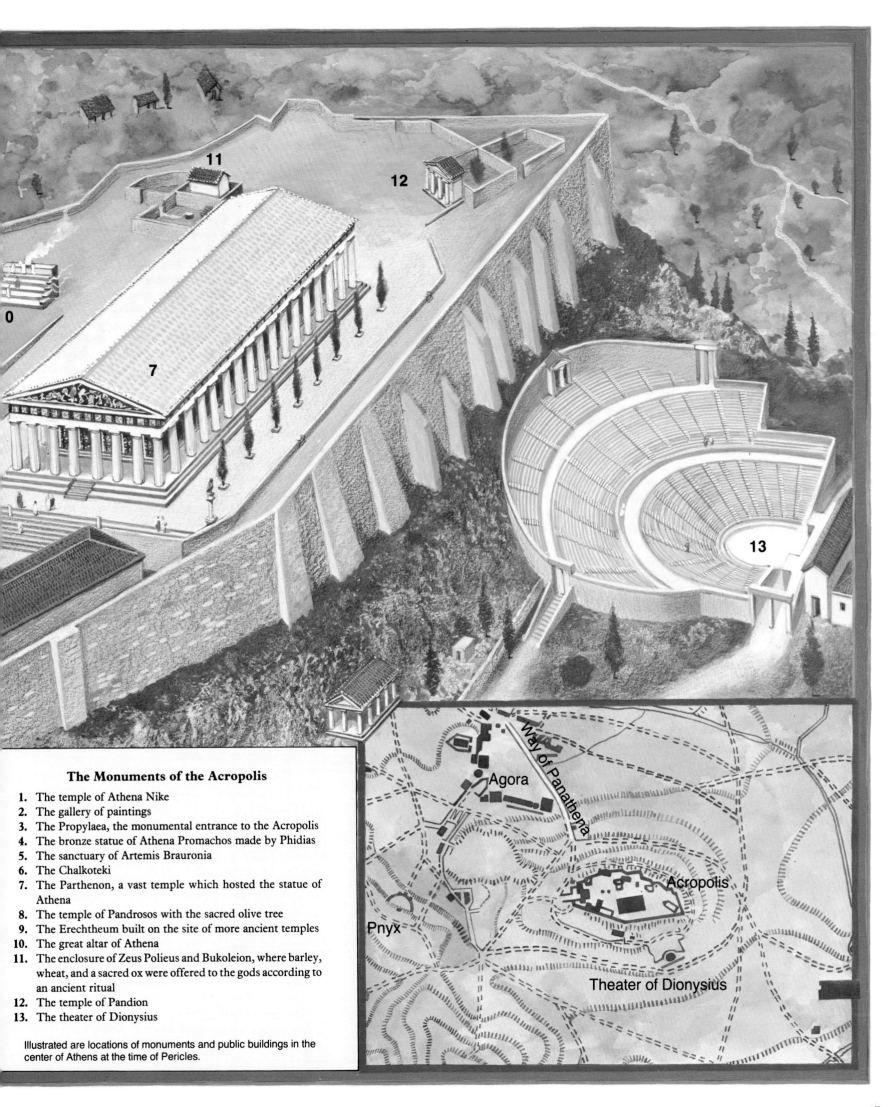

The Monuments of the Acropolis

1. The temple of Athena Nike
2. The gallery of paintings
3. The Propylaea, the monumental entrance to the Acropolis
4. The bronze statue of Athena Promachos made by Phidias
5. The sanctuary of Artemis Brauronia
6. The Chalkoteki
7. The Parthenon, a vast temple which hosted the statue of Athena
8. The temple of Pandrosos with the sacred olive tree
9. The Erechtheum built on the site of more ancient temples
10. The great altar of Athena
11. The enclosure of Zeus Polieus and Bukoleion, where barley, wheat, and a sacred ox were offered to the gods according to an ancient ritual
12. The temple of Pandion
13. The theater of Dionysius

Illustrated are locations of monuments and public buildings in the center of Athens at the time of Pericles.

THE GREEKS IN THE MEDITERRANEAN

Greater Greece and Sicily

The Greek colonies became more splendid and richer in art and culture than Greece itself. The first colonies established by the Greeks were Pithecusae (on today's island of Ischia) and Cyme in the Campania region. The towns of Messene, Rhegion, Leontini, Catana, and Himera were founded shortly afterward. The settlers made wise use of the resources of the territory (tin, copper, and bronze). In a short time, they gained control over much of the sea traffic going west through the Straits of Messene. Other Greek populations carried on the colonization process. They were Megarians,

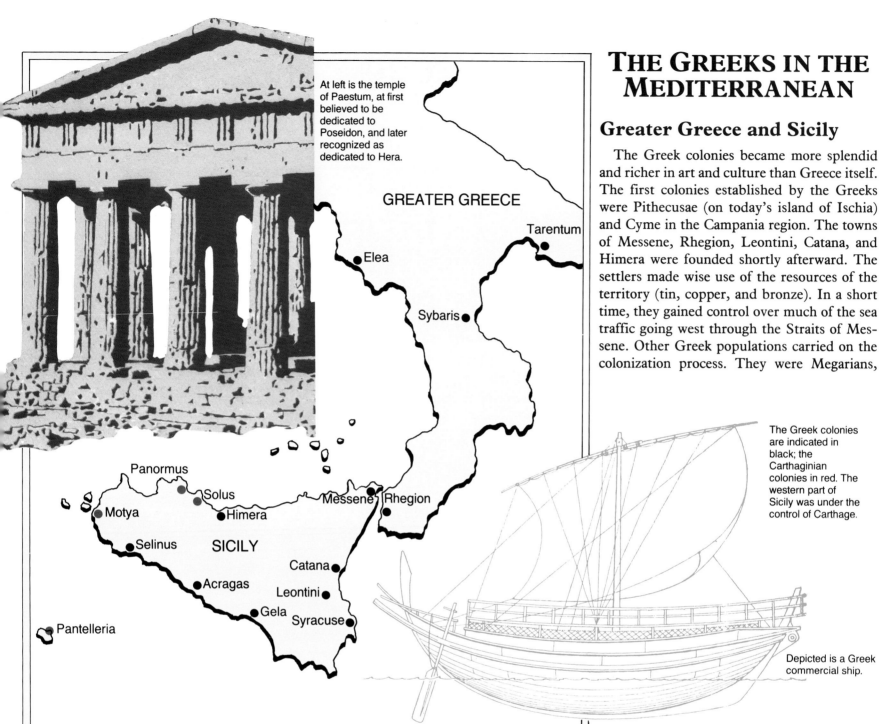

At left is the temple of Paestum, at first believed to be dedicated to Poseidon, and later recognized as dedicated to Hera.

GREATER GREECE

Tarentum

Elea

Sybaris

Panormus

Solus

Motya

Himera

Messene Rhegion

Selinus

SICILY

Catana

Acragas

Leontini

Gela

Syracuse

Pantelleria

The Greek colonies are indicated in black; the Carthaginian colonies in red. The western part of Sicily was under the control of Carthage.

Depicted is a Greek commercial ship.

SICILY, RULED BY THE GREAT TYRANTS

A new form of government originated in Sicily. It was halfway between the government of the Greek polis and that of the eastern states. Its head was a lord who ruled over the court and the army. This form of government was called tyranny. The tyrant Dionysius ruled over a large town close to today's Syracuse. Immigrants and mercenary soldiers found work in Syracuse and were granted the same political rights as the citizens of the town. Actually, all citizens were subject to the tyrants, even if the tyrants had the approval of the majority of people and were opposed to the aristocratic groups. The latter wanted to revive oligarchic power, although with such a system the various factions were in constant disagreement with each other.

Not only did Syracuse become the largest city in the Greek world, but it was actually the capital of a vast territory. This territory came to include most of Sicily and numerous towns of southern Italy. Its influence was felt throughout the Mediterranean, all the way to the area where Venice was to develop in later times. Syracuse was always at war with Carthage, which was to become the most important naval power in the Mediterranean prior to Rome. This constant state of war, both against Carthage and against the Etruscans in Italy, together with the desire of Syracuse to impose its power over various Greek towns, was one of the reasons which justified the need for a tyrannical government.

Corinthians, Achaeans, Spartans, and Cretans. In Sicily, they founded important towns such as Syracuse, Gela, Acragas, and Selinus; in Greater Greece they founded Tarentum, Elea, and Sybaris.

The Coast of Gaul

The Phocaeans, who had elongated and swift ships propelled by fifty rowers, reached the coast of Gaul. There, around 600 B.C., they founded the town of Massilia. The area was rich in tin, coral, and salt, and was also in a favorable location for trade. The Phocaeans were actually going in search of locations where they could sell goods. In Massilia, they entered into direct commercial competition with the Etruscans. The latter had already established an ongoing exchange of metals and ceramics with the populations of the Languedoc, Catalogne, and Provence regions. Even Carthage, which had dominion over trade in the western Mediterranean,

The Greeks had fruitful contacts with other peoples throughout the Mediterranean. Besides trading goods, they exchanged art and other products of their culture. 1) Trading of grains in the harbor of Massilia; 2) Greek merchants offer a vase made in Greece to a Celtic aristocrat; 3) Greek ships; 4) Greek chariots; 5) a sea battle between Greeks and Carthaginians; 6) exchange of handicrafts between Greeks and Etruscans.

was affected by the presence of the Greeks. An important military event was the battle of Alalia (around 540 B.C.). The Etruscans and Carthaginians fought successfully together against the Greeks in order to defend their commercial dominion from the influence of the Phocaeans who had settled in Corsica.

Massilia gradually obtained a vast maritime empire. Among its numerous colonies were Olbia, Anthibes, Nice, Agde, Le Bruc, and other coastal towns. In this way, in spite of its very limited territory, Massilia was able to spread its culture and its commercial products along the valley of the Rhone, up to the heart of the Celtic territory.

Greeks and Carthaginians in Iberia

Both Greeks and Carthaginians had had commercial bases in Iberia for a long time. In some cases, settlers came from their mother countries to create colonies. The Greek people were essentially merchants and established more or less permanent stopovers (emporias) or utilized preexisting ones. They would exchange their merchandise and leave again with a load of silver and other precious metals. A permanent colony was founded with the intervention of the people from Massilia on the Spanish coast north of the Ebro River. It was called Emporion (today's Ampurias).

The Mediterranean and Europe

From 800 B.C. to 300 B.C., trade activities and the settlement of colonies caused an encounter of peoples and cultures which had an influence on the Mediterranean and on European civilization. The expansion of Greece and Carthage triggered extremely fast historical development. A common heritage of art, style, and values developed. This gave great stimulus to the growth of local cultures, such as those of the Italic populations or the Iberian-Punic populations. The growth of this culture positively influenced the temperate regions of Europe. It caused great change in the Celtic world.

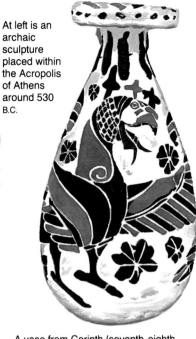

At left is an archaic sculpture placed within the Acropolis of Athens around 530 B.C.

A vase from Corinth (seventh-eighth century B.C.) is pictured. Due to oriental influence, the Greek vase painters enriched their works with new decorative patterns such as that of a griffin.

A temple is shown under construction. The heavy blocks of stone were transported with the help of special machinery. A winch was used to lift the sections of columns, and scaffolding allowed work on upper levels. *Top insert:* The technique employed in lifting heavy stone blocks in order to position them securely, one beside the other, made use of vertical and horizontal wedges. The tools used in sculpting stone were, as they are today, hammers and chisels, used first in rough-shaping and then in fine finishing work.

THE ART OF GREECE

Greek art is divided into three periods—archaic, classic, and Hellenistic. The most famous is the classical period, which dates from the end of the Persian war (480 B.C.) to the invasion of the Persian Empire by Alexander the Great (333-323 B.C.). Victory over the Persians played a major role in forming the mentality that created the art of the early and mature classical periods. On the other hand, the conquest of Alexander and the spread of Greek culture in the east marked the final steps in the process of social and emotional transformation. This began with the Peloponnesian War and in time destroyed the principles of classical art.

From the Archaic Period to the Early Classical Period

The classical period in Greek art was preceded by the archaic period, which dated from the seventh century B.C. to shortly before the Persian wars. This period is characterized by a search for universal order. The statues seem to be untouched by human events. On the other hand, the statues of the first classical period (480-450 B.C.) tend to be dramatic and associated with the times.

The Greek artists believed that the basis of human expression was the ethos (the nature of people and their traditions, habits, and morals) and the pathos (people's spontaneous reaction to experience). One of the best examples of expression of ethos is in the work of art, the Charioteer of Delphi. The serious, aristocratic self-control of this figure is the ideal representa-

tion of victory after a chariot race. But even during the early classical period, there was a belief that harmony and order could be found in movement. Thus, sculpted or painted figures were depicted as reacting, moving, or thinking.

In sculpture, an aspect of composition called rythmos became predominant. It froze movement, capturing an entire action within an instant. A typical example is the *Discobolus,* a work of the sculptor Myron, in which a discus thrower is represented a moment before his throw.

From the Classical Period to the Hellenistic Period

The value of symmetry was always appreciated in Greek art, and the classical period was the time of its highest expression. A work had to be composed of clearly definable parts, capable of bringing opposite forces into harmony. Symmetry is very finely expressed in the Parthenon.

The building expresses trust in people, and its art expresses the certainty that human reason will prevail and perfect the world. Its architecture and its sculptures, the work of the artist Pheidias and his students, celebrate the values of the city and community.

The combination of the Dorian and Ionic orders was one of the elements used to express the quality of Athens in the time of Pericles. The Dorian order was associated with the solid simplicity of the descendants of Hercules in the Peloponnese, while the Ionic order expressed luxury and refinement. It was only natural that Pericles wanted the two orders to be present and brought into harmony in the art of Athens. The art which followed the Peloponnesian War (from 431 to 404 B.C.) reflected the disintegration of this mentality and the disillusionment with the values of the polis. The primary sculptors of this time were Praxiteles, Scopa, and Lysippus.

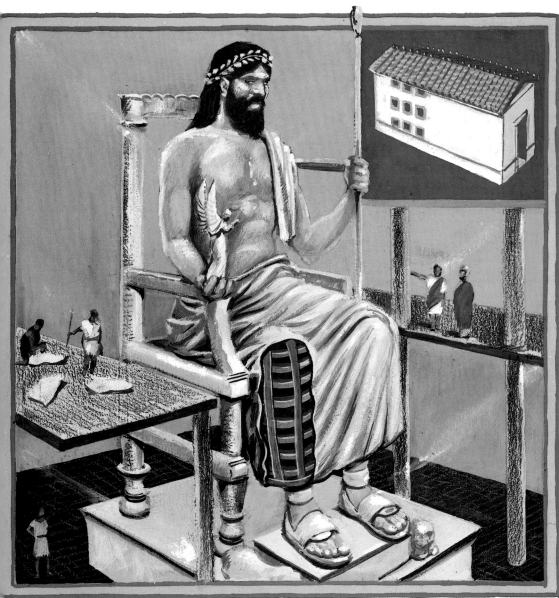

The *Discobolus* by the sculptor Myron illustrates the great sense of movement expressed by artists of the early classical period.

The bronze *Charioteer of Delphi* (478-474 B.C.) wears the clothing typical of his profession. It is a tunic, belted in a particular way. The statue is a superb example of the nobility of the human figure as it was expressed in classical art.

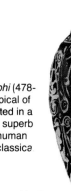

A vase with red figures on a black background (Eretria, approximately 430 B.C.) is shown. It is the work of a great painter, and it depicts a woman holding a ribbon in one hand and a box in the other.

At Olympia, in the workshop of Pheidias, some artisans apply the last gold plate to the statue of Zeus which will be installed in the Temple of Zeus. Today, this statue is lost, but it can be envisioned thanks to written testimony and to some archaeological finds. It was built of ivory and gold plates applied to a wooden internal frame. *Top insert:* The workshop which Pheidias constructed in order to build this statue was situated in the same direction as the temple, and the light from its windows entered at the same angle.

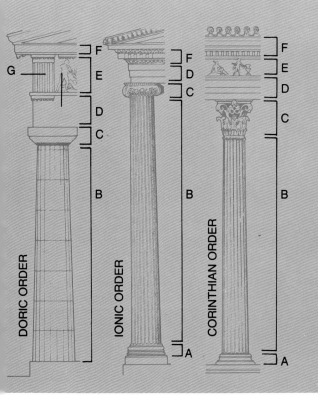

The Architectural Orders

Greek architecture was composed of vertical elements, the columns, which supported horizontal elements, the trabeations. Trabeations were lintels (**D**), friezes (**E**), and cornices (**F**). Buildings were placed in one of the three classical orders.

THE DORIC ORDER is the most ancient. Its footless columns possess twenty grooves; the length of their shafts (**B**) is four to six times the diameter of their bases. The frieze has vertical grooves called triglyphs (**G**) alternating with ornamental bas-reliefs called metope (**H**).

THE IONIC ORDER with its typical voluted capitals originated in Asia Minor in the sixth century B.C. Its columns possess twenty-four grooves, divided by cinctures; the total length of their shafts is generally nine times the diameter of the base of their shafts.

THE CORINTHIAN ORDER possesses a typical capital decorated with acanthus leaves. The lintel is almost always surmounted by friezes. Usually the height of the columns is ten times the diameter of the base of the shafts.

In the following centuries, art increasingly reflected the experience of each person as an individual and was called Hellenistic. Pathos received more attention than ethos which no longer expressed the ideals of the community. The artists were exploring personal emotions such as pain, tenderness, and humor. In seeking refuge in gesture and elegance of shapes, the artists were expressing their wishes to withdraw from the intellectual and political hardship of the period.

Building Techniques

The Greek people had acquired great skill in building. This is evident in their temples, which are the principal objects of Greek architecture, in their city planning, and in their public buildings such as theaters, stadiums, and gymnasiums. The techniques and methods of construction were highly developed. Plans were drawn up by workers who each had a specialized responsibility. Machines for building included wheels, rollers, levers, winches, and runners.

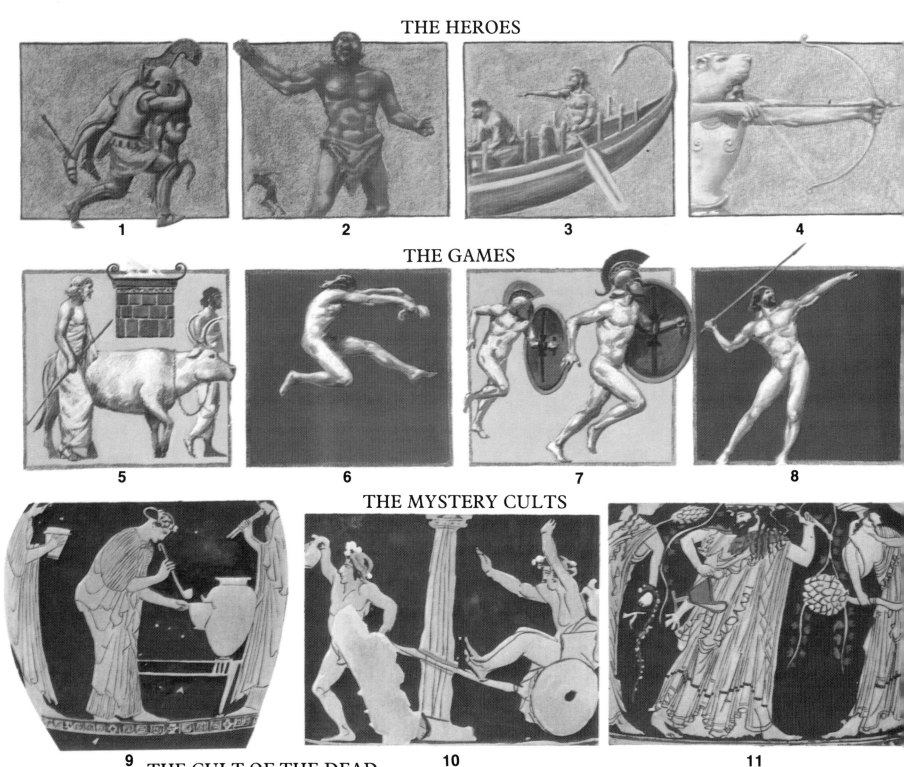

THE HEROES

1   **2**   **3**   **4**

THE GAMES

5   **6**   **7**   **8**

THE MYSTERY CULTS

9   **10**   **11**

THE CULT OF THE DEAD

12

THE HEROES: **1)** Ajax carries Achilles. These are two heroes from the *Iliad,* famous for their courage in battle. **2)** Ulysses, from the *Odyssey,* the hero of human intelligence, escapes from the giant Polyphemus. **3)** Theseus, the mythical king of Athens, established order and unity on his return to his homeland. **4)** Shown is a typical representationof Hercules, the invincible hero who was made a divinity after his death. Here, he is clothed in the skin of a lion.

THE GAMES: **5)** An ox is brought to be sacrificed prior to the opening of the games. **6)** The long jump is depicted. **7)** A footrace is run with helmets and shields. **8)** The javelin throw is pictured.

THE MYSTERY CULTS: **9)** The cult of Dionysus inspired the figures on ancient vases. A priestess distributes wine. **10)** Two young men carry a special vessel for the new wine. **(11)** Dionysus holds a cup in his hand.

THE CULT OF THE DEAD: **12)** At a funeral banquet, the son of the dead offers milk, flatbread, and other food, while a lamb is readied for sacrifice.

Opposite page: Mount Olympus is pictured with its gods. There are twelve principal deities—Zeus, the strongest of all the gods; Hera, his wife; Poseidon, the god of the sea; Athena, the protectress of fortresses and towns as well as the goddess of wisdom; Apollo, the god of youth and the healing song; Artemis, the goddess of animals and wilderness as well as of the hunt; Aphrodite, the goddess of love; Hermes, the god of cleverness and the gods' speedy messenger; Demeter, the goddess of crops; Dionysus, the god of wine and the ecstasy of intoxication; Hephaestus, the artisan god and lord of the fire; and Ares, the god of war.

THE RELIGION OF THE GREEKS

Usually Greek religion is identified with the gods of Mount Olympus. In reality, other deities were also respected. Each family, for example, could have its own god. Each town had its own god, as did each occupation or art. Failure to respect the deities could result in the grave accusation of impiety. The Greeks also held many sites, animals, and plants as sacred.

The Underworld and the Cult of the Dead

Some deities inhabited Hades, the obscure underworld. The cult connected to this universe of darkness is rich and full of the fearful things the Greeks thought waited them in the afterlife. Many rituals were aimed at avoiding the possible revenge of the dead.

The Oracles: An Answer from the Gods

The Greek people were anxious to know about their futures. They particularly looked for the signs of divine fury which they tended to see in unusual or exceptional events or in omens connected to natural phenomena such as eclipses of the sun, thunder, or lightning. An ability which had been respected since ancient times was that of prophesying, which was the skill of communicating the will of the gods to people. The most famous oracle was the priestess of Delphi in the temple of Apollo. This attempt to see into the future and to understand the will of the gods showed the desire of the Greek people to establish communications with the gods.

Heroes and Games

Men who had done great deeds or the sons of the gods were highly respected by the Greeks. These were the heroes, the most famous of whom was Hercules. Athletic competitions were often a part of the cult of heroes and were not merely sports events.

The Myth

The word *mythos* means "word" and comes from the Indo-European term *mudh*, which means "to reflect" or "to consider." The most ancient texts used the word *mythos* to indicate a story concerning the gods.

Homer, who probably lived in the eighth century B.C., wrote two great poems—the *Iliad*, a grand epic about the Trojan War, and the *Odyssey*, which narrates the deeds of Telemakhos and Ulysses. In these poems, the gods are depicted as forces that intervene in the lives of people. Hesiod probably lived in the 700s B.C. He wrote *The Works and Days*, a poem dedicated to the earth, and *Theogony*, which tells of the origins of gods and earthly things. Homer and Hesiod organized a collection of myths. Poets were to sing of these myths in later times, and they were to be the substance of the famous Greek tragedies.

In following centuries, religious thought, philosophical research, and literary activities dealt with the myths, at times criticizing them. Starting from the late seventh century B.C., philosophy attempted to provide a rational explanation of the world. The word *mythos* was to be replaced by *logos*, also meaning "word" and "thought." The logos was considered the spiritual principle which permeates all things. Plato was to give a new interpretation of the myths in order to provide people with a religious, moral, and political education.

Until the coming of Christianity, Homer was considered a poet who expressed, with his myths, a revelation taken from a divine source. Thus, the myths introduced people to religious mysteries. Later, myths were regarded in various ways, either as the poetic expressions of historical events or as a means of understanding natural phenomena.

Today, myths are seen as sacred stories which poetically express beliefs concerning fundamental situations related to humans—their origin, death, hope, and the relationship between humans and divinity. Myths do not relate a story according to actual history, though sometimes they originated from real events. On the contrary, myths express a consciousness of the human condition, a reflection of a truth that goes beyond history.

HERMES
ZEUS
HERA
DEMETER
ATHENA
POSEIDON
APHRODITE
APOLLO
ARTEMIS
HEPHAESTUS
ARES
DIONYSUS
MOUNT OLYMPUS

The Mysteries

The mysteries were secret ceremonies of very ancient origin in which the wisdom of myths was revealed. The message told of the possibility of a new life after death. This life was not that of Hades, which was sad and dark. Instead, it was a peaceful existence. The most well-known mystery cult was the cult of Dionysus.

The Gods of Mount Olympus

On Mount Olympus, the gods lived in a world ruled by Zeus. The difficult relationship between people and the unpredictable gods was often an object of reflection.

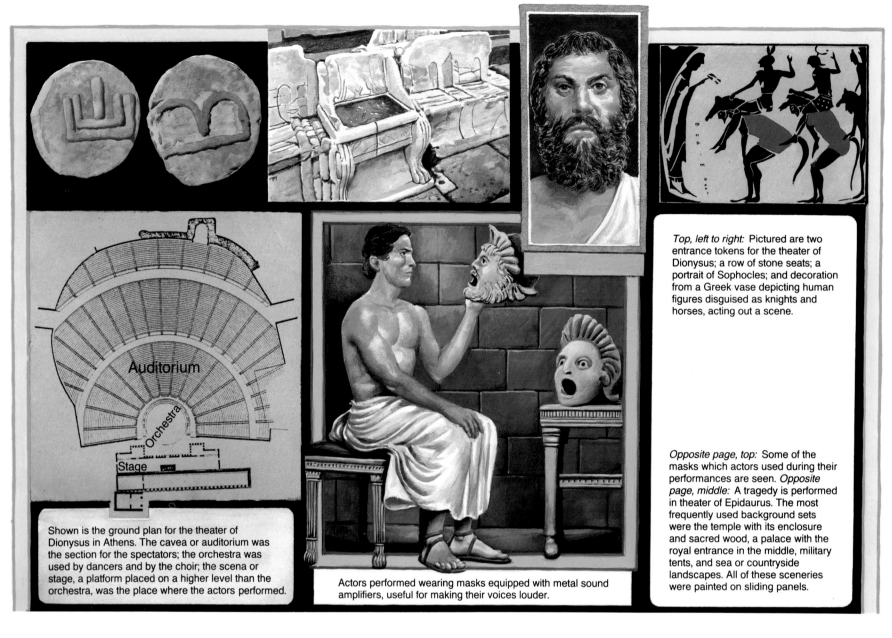

Top, left to right: Pictured are two entrance tokens for the theater of Dionysus; a row of stone seats; a portrait of Sophocles; and decoration from a Greek vase depicting human figures disguised as knights and horses, acting out a scene.

Opposite page, top: Some of the masks which actors used during their performances are seen. *Opposite page, middle:* A tragedy is performed in theater of Epidaurus. The most frequently used background sets were the temple with its enclosure and sacred wood, a palace with the royal entrance in the middle, military tents, and sea or countryside landscapes. All of these sceneries were painted on sliding panels.

Auditorium

Orchestra

Stage

Shown is the ground plan for the theater of Dionysus in Athens. The cavea or auditorium was the section for the spectators; the orchestra was used by dancers and by the choir; the scena or stage, a platform placed on a higher level than the orchestra, was the place where the actors performed.

Actors performed wearing masks equipped with metal sound amplifiers, useful for making their voices louder.

GREEK THEATER

The Greeks Invent Tragedies and Comedies

The Greek people invented a great form of artistic expression capable of involving and deeply moving the audience. It was the tragedy. Later on, the comedy was invented. These two artistic forms of theater developed further and, with some variations, have reached modern times.

The Origins of Tragedy: A Religious Ceremony

According to tradition, the first tragedy was played in Athens during the sixty-first Olympic Games (536-533 B.C.). In front of the audience gathered in the cavea, a sacrifice was offered to Dionysus, followed by dances. Lyrics sung by the choir alternated with mixed parts, where the actor could either interrelate with the chorus or recite a monologue. These pieces were generally preceded by a prologue and by an entrance song performed by the choir. The event ended with a closing song. The choir played the most important role in the show. Later, the parts performed by the choir tended to become detached from the plot of the narration and were basically used as an expression of the feelings of the playwright.

Tragedy as an Expression of the Polis

The performance of the tragedy, organized by the government of the polis, was a public ritual which was celebrated during the festivals in honor of Dionysus. In the fifth century, the Athenian tragic drama took on all the grandeur of this artistic form. The purpose of the drama was to present the citizens with a performance which would make them reflect upon their experiences within the social community.

ANTIGONE BY SOPHOCLES

In Thebes, the two brothers, Eteocles and Polynices, fought for this kingdom to the point of killing each other. Creon, their uncle, ascended the throne and forbade the burying of the body of Polynices. Polynices's sister, Antigone, who believed in the religious tradition that the dead could not find peace until they were buried, disobeyed the order of the king and buried her brother. The king delivered a cruel sentence—Antigone was to be buried alive. Antigone's

The Tragedy as an Expression of Human Drama

The tragedies of the three great Greek dramatists, Aeschylus, Sophocles, and Euripides, were not simply an expression of social life in the polis. All of the major themes which were at the basis of Greek civilization, such as the search for identity and the passions and doubts of people, were present in the tragedies.

The Comedy

The birth of comedy was also related to religious rituals, part of the cult of Baccus and Dionysus. In Athens, the performance of comedies always attracted large crowds. Audience members, numbering up to fifteen thousand, would take active part applauding and roaring. The most important writer of Greek comedy was Aristophanes (448-388 B.C.).

Later, Menander (342-291 B.C.) created a sort of comedy which dealt with various characters—the miserly, the peevish, the servant, and so forth.

The Great Tragedy Writers

AESCHYLUS (524-456 B.C.) wrote *Prometheus Bound.* Prometheus, a demi-god, had been punished because he had taught the use

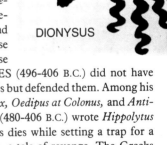

DIONYSUS

of fire. SOPHOCLES (496-406 B.C.) did not have blind faith in the gods but defended them. Among his plays are *Oedipus Rex, Oedipus at Colonus,* and *Antigone.* EURIPIDES (480-406 B.C.) wrote *Hippolytus* in which Hippolytus dies while setting a trap for a goddess, and *Medea,* a tale of revenge. The Greeks believed the gods capable of doing evil and that death put an end to everything.

fiancee, Haemon, the son of Creon, followed the girl into her tomb without his father's knowledge. Later, Creon, seized by doubt, ordered that the tomb be reopened. He found Antigone, who had just committed suicide, and his son who killed himself in front of him. Eurydice, his mother, was overwhelmed by grief and also committed suicide.

Thales was the founder of the first Greek school of philosophy and was well known among his contemporaries because he predicted the eclipse of the sun during a battle on May 28, 585 B.C. He thought that the world was floating, suspended in water, which was the primeval substance of life.

PYTHAGORAS

The school of Pythagoras studied mathematics and intellectual training which developed clarity of thought. Also, geometry was organized into theorems and proofs. Arithmetic was the study of proportions, and music was translated into numbers. The students of Pythagoras also studied astronomy, and they concluded that the earth is a revolving sphere.

DEMOCRITOS

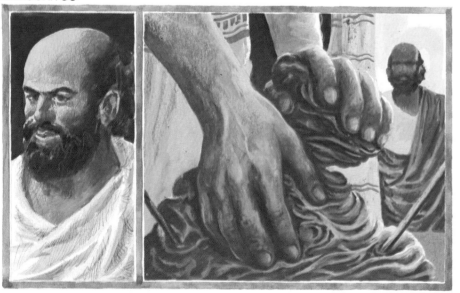

Democritos formulated a theory that the world was composed only of atoms and empty space, and that the atoms united and separated according to an internal requirement. The hypotheses of Democritos were among the most famous in science and remained a reference point for the scholars of later times.

GREEK THOUGHT

The First School of Philosophy

In the sixth century, a certain political stability was accompanied in the Greek world by economic prosperity. In Ionia in particular, such peace generated a great cultural liveliness. In Miletus, the southernmost of the Ionic towns, the first school of philosophy flourished.

Thales and his Disciples

Thales of Miletus, 640-548 B.C., was the first master to found a Greek school of philosophy. He introduced mathematics and astronomy into Greece. He was looking for the primeval substance from which everything derived, and he thought he had found it in the element of water. His vision of matter was very practical but didn't completely exclude the presence of God or of an eternal life force.

Pythagoras and His School

Pythagoras, of Samos, an island near Miletus, also lived in the sixth century (from 580 to 500 B.C.) and taught in Croton in southern Italy. He created a community of followers, men and women, who used the intellect as a source of spiritual purification. Pythagoras was involved in mathematics and natural sciences. In his opinion, harmony was the ideal condition of the world and was attained by keeping just proportions of all things. The school of Pythagoras also strived to discover the primal element of reality. The last followers of Pythagoras stated that everything was composed of numbers which they considered indivisible units or atoms. In this way, a new school called the atomistic school was born.

Heraclitus of Ephesos

Heraclitus was an original thinker, and his teachings reached their height around 500 B.C. He lived on a mountain and looked for the one idea which would be capable of explaining everything. His thought was based on the intuition that constant change ruled the world.

Parmenides of Elea

Parmenides lived in Elea in the Lucania region of Italy. Unlike Heraclitus, who insisted on the idea that everything was in motion, Parmenides was an advocate of the idea that things resisted change.

Democritos of Abdera

Abdera was an Ionic colony of Thrace. Here lived Democritos, an exponent of the atomistic school which developed from the school of Pythagoras. Democritos, however, never founded a school. He believed that the knowledge which is acquired based on sensory perceptions is illusory, and the only certainty comes from the domain of thought. According to Democritos, the world (including people) was made of atoms which could be neither created nor destroyed but merely changed.

The Sophists

In the second half of the fifth century B.C., Athens became the cultural capital of the Greek world and the center of a vast intellectual movement which was characterized by faith in the strength of human thought. The *Sophists,* a word which means "masters of wisdom," were an important element in this movement. Among the teachers was Protagoras, who lived a generation before Socrates and declared that humans were the measure of all things. He negated the existence of an absolute truth but stated that there were only specific truths which were valid for some people in particular situations.

Socrates

Socrates investigated human nature, looking for true wisdom. But he soon arrived at the conclusion that he could only ask questions; that his wisdom was that he didn't know anything and his only teaching was about the art of examining ideas. The true virtue, for him, was reached through the search for reason which opened the way to universal truth, the conceptual truth.

Plato

Plato (427-347 B.C.) founded an institution called the Academy in Athens. It was a kind of philosophical fraternity to which both men and women were admitted. For Plato, philosophy was the science of ideas, which are the original and eternal models of all reality. He believed in the existence of a god who created all things and to whom people's souls are attracted through love. The supreme idea of Plato is the concept of good, the capacity of loving truth and acting in accordance with truth.

Aristotle

Aristotle (384-322 B.C.) was an illustrious disciple of Plato. He was claimed to have taught Alexander the Great and then returned to Athens to begin a school dedicated to Apollo Lyceum, the god of shepherds. The school was called the Lyceum and was founded by Alexander. According to Aristotle, humans had an active, rational capability which allowed them to partake in the creativity of the universe, or god, which was the cause and effect that set everything in motion. Art and thought must grasp the essential form of everything. This form is not impossible to discern but is found in matter through sensory perception. The concept of good, recognized by virtue, is happiness. Politics was, for Plato, the science of collective happiness. The main characteristic of Aristotle's work is the systematic ordering of all the knowledge of his time.

Aristotle's philosophy tried to explain the fundamentals of reality. He defined the way thought worked, and he introduced syllogism. Syllogism is reasoning which allows one to draw certain conclusions starting from probable premises. In this illustration, starting from the two premises that "all the fruits are edible" and "this apple is a fruit," it can be concluded that "this apple can be eaten."

The personality of Socrates was described with admiration by his students, among them Plato and Xenophon. A part of Socrates's method was to invite anyone into discussion. In particular, he loved to teach young people. He used a method which was called Maieutic, which means the art of midwifery. Just as a midwife helps a child to come into the world, Socrates, with his continuous questions, helped youths bring to light the truth they had inside.

PLATO

Plato founded the Academy, a meeting place for young scholars and philosophers. At the center of his teachings, Plato placed the examination of the relationship between human experience and ideas.

ARISTOTLE

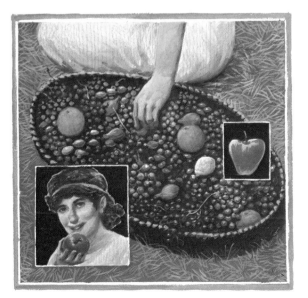

THE EMPIRE OF ALEXANDER

When the crisis of the polis (frequent warfare due to overpopulation) became worse in Greece, the peripheral regions acquired greater importance. The power of Sparta over the Greek towns was briefly replaced by the power of Thebes and Boetia. More to the north, however, a kingdom called Macedonia was developing which was to conquer all of the Greek world and other territories.

Philip II of Macedonia Conquers Greece

Since 360 B.C., Philip II, son of Argaeus, ruled over Macedonia. He succeeded in strengthening his kingdom by gathering all the nobles into the court and by reorganizing his army in a more efficient way (the well-known Macedonian phalanx). Philip intruded in the constant fights between the poleis, allying with various contenders, and eventually imposed his dominion over Greece. He unified the Greek world but not the way the polis would have wished. Athens resisted him at the urging of Demosthenes but was defeated. This defeat marked the end of the independence of the Greek towns.

Alexander Conquers the Persian Empire

After Philip's assassination, his son Alexander ascended to the throne. He brutally crushed the last attempts of the poleis to regain their independence and punished Thebes with total destruction. Then, he carried out his father's project—conquering Persia and creating a vast empire from the Aegean to the Oceanos, the mythical river which the Greeks thought surrounded the earth. In 334 B.C., Alexander launched an attack upon Persia and conquered its empire. He ultimately reached the Indus Valley in India before turning back to Mesopotamia.

The Imperial Design of Alexander

Alexander placed the capital of his empire in Babylon. He believed that he was endowed with a special religious authority as had been confirmed by Egyptian priests who had proclaimed him the son of god and the successor to the

Above is a Macedonian soldier.

The Macedonian infantry, which was long considered invincible, was organized into a phalanx. It was composed of eight thousand infantrymen lined up in sixteen rows.

1) Shown is a coin of the time of Philip, with the image of a knight on a horse, issued between 350 and 330 B.C. 2) Shown is a coin with a knight from Paeonia (a region in northern Macedonia) who belonged to the cavalry of Alexander. 3) This coin was stamped in Alexandria, Egypt. 4) Pictured is a gold medallion found in Abusir in Egypt with the image of Alexander, like a hero, with his horse, Bucephalus. 5-6) Shown is a coin minted in Babylon soon after the victory of Alexander over the Persian Porus.

Depicted is the route of the campaign of Alexander and the extent of his empire, stretching from Greece to Ind The European and Asian worlds were closely connec and opened for communication.

pharaohs. Alexander valued knowledge and scientific curiosity and understood their political value. For this reason, a group of scholars accompanied him on his expeditions. They had the tasks of measuring distances, describing the different countries, and studying the customs and medical practices of the various cultures. He tried to unite the different populations of his empire, and he favored the union of the East and the West, but this union was never achieved. Ambassadors, as well as Greek, Persian, Celtic, Spanish, Roman, and Carthaginian merchants congregated at the court at Babylon, but each of these populations was still attached to its own traditions. These countries were highly suspicious of the barbarian eastern countries.

Above is a Persian soldier.

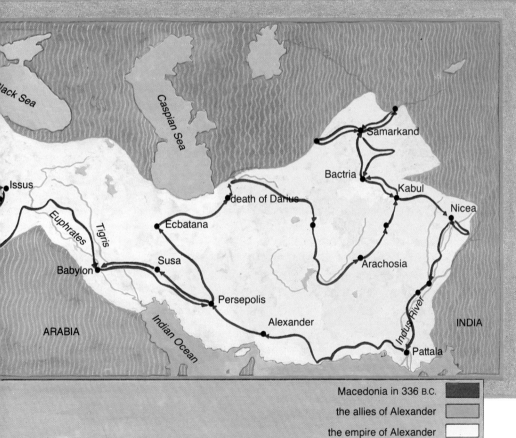
Macedonia in 336 B.C.
the allies of Alexander
the empire of Alexander

In the Greek towns of Asia Minor, the Hellenistic tradition continued, even after the death of Alexander. Pictured is a meeting of some members of the boule or council in the council room of the small town of Priene in Ionia.

The Heritage of Alexander in Europe and the Middle East

Upon the death of Alexander in 323 B.C., his generals fought each other, then divided the territory of the empire between them. Three great states emerged. One was Macedonia, and also included the Greek world. One was Egypt, and the last was the Middle East.

Hellenistic Monarchy

A Hellenistic monarchy was a form of government in which the powers of the state were in the hands of the king who ruled by the strength of his army. Under the power of the king, the difference between Greek and non-Greek citizens disappeared. The ideal of the unity of humanity was born. Different peoples could live in political harmony because they found the symbol of their unity and a guarantee for good government in the leadership of their king. The king became a god who was worshipped. After Alexander, the Hellenistic kings were to be listed among the gods of the Greek towns.

ETRUSCAN ROME AND THE LEGEND OF THE OUSTING OF THE KINGS

Urban life in Etruscan Rome is depicted. *Top insert:* An Etruscan king *(seated)* is pictured with the symbols of power which Rome was to inherit. They were a curule seat and a scepter. Two Roman officers are seen holding fasces, bundles of rods with an ax which represented authority.

The Civilization of the Etruscans

The Etruscan civilization had developed in the central part of the Italian peninsula, beginning around 750 B.C. It was the result of the evolution of local populations and apparently colonists from Asia Minor at the beginning stages of the Iron Age. The center of development of the Etruscan world was Tuscany, but soon the Etruscans spread past the Apennines into the Po Valley and to the south toward the territories of greater Greece. They were skilled sailors and merchants and were very good at smelting and crafting metals, including iron. The Etruscans were the first to build towns in the regions they inhabited. Their civilization involved rich religious tradition. The Etruscans believed that the acts of people were sacred and had to conform to the design of the gods.

Etruscans and Latins in Rome

During their migration to the south, the Etruscans came into contact with the Latin populations which inhabited today's Latium. They didn't succeed in conquering the region and had to be satisfied with gaining control of the main trade routes with the rich Greek territories. At points along the Tiber River atop several hills, Latin villages had existed for several centuries and eventually unified. This was the first nucleus of the urban center of Rome. The Etruscans settled as merchants in Rome. They later seized power, and it is probable that three Etruscan kings ruled the city—Servius Tulius, Tarquinius Priscus, and Tarquinius Superbus, the Proud. The presence of the Etruscans had introduced a high degree of civilization in the ancient Latin nucleus. The population had grown, and numerous public buildings existed. On the other hand, there were tensions between the Etruscans and Latins. In the sixth century, opposition against King Tarquinius the Proud grew, and he was ousted.

SPQR

S.P.Q.R. is the Latin abbreviation for "Senatus Populusque Romanus," which means "the Senate and the Roman people." This slogan expressed trust in people and in the Roman institutions.

THE BIRTH OF ROMAN CIVILIZATION

The Romans Found the Republic

Although the Roman people were hostile to Tarquinius and his family, other external factors also led to the fall of the king. Around 509 B.C., the Etruscan king Porsenna of the city of Clusium invaded Latium, seized Rome, and ousted the family of Tarquinius. Porsenna was based in Rome for his military expeditions throughout Latium but did not rule the city itself. The Romans, without a king, gave their city an aristocratic government in which most of the political positions were in the hands of the patricians.

The patricians were the most powerful Latins in Rome. They were the men who, at the moment of the shift from monarchy to republic, held the most important magistratures and also had some religious functions.

For a long time, the organization of Rome was similar to that of the Greek city-states. Around the second century B.C., Rome was still an independent and sovereign civic community where city and countryside were tightly bound by common laws. In order to enjoy the full political rights and laws of Rome, one had to be a citizen.

The Periods of Roman History

The Republican Age (500 B.C.-27 B.C.) started with the ousting of the kings and lasted five centuries. In this period, Rome strengthened its political institutions and its way of life and expanded throughout Europe and the Mediterranean.

The Imperial Age was characterized by the presence of the emperor. The various men who held this position varied greatly in their leadership capabilities and power. One period of the Imperial Age was the Principate (from 27 B.C. to the Antonine Emperors). In the Principate, the Republican magistratures were kept intact, and the figure of the "Princeps" was added. The Princeps was the emperor and the first citizen. He ruled with the collaboration of the senate. In spite of some military conquests, these two centuries were a time of peace. Another part of the Imperial Age was Dominatus (from A.D. 193 to the time of Constantine the Great, A.D. 324-337) in which the emperors were almost always elected by the army and ruled without the support of the senate.

THE INHERITANCE LEFT BY ROME

Rome was a powerful and often bloodthirsty civilization that blazed new trails in history.

The Pax Deorum

The first Romans had received from the Etruscans a deep sense of history, a sense of sacredness in which great importance was given to their ancestors. They believed that the consequence of good deeds could be inherited and that errors and faults had to be eliminated. The Romans believed in the existence of a great alliance between the gods and Rome. It was called the Pax Deorum (the peace of the gods). This was the expression of a new trust in the relationship between gods and people, an innovation differing from the oriental traditions and even from early Greek wisdom. This belief that the gods supported Rome made the Romans confident as they embarked in enterprises and expanded throughout the world. Moreover, it provided the Romans with a great sense of tolerance toward foreigners and even enemies. After having been conquered, some could become part of the Roman world and acquire Roman citizenship. However, others were enslaved or sacrificed in gladitorial combat for amusement of bloodthirsty crowds. One thing not tolerated was impiety, which means public disrespect for the gods of Rome. Impious individuals were often persecuted.

Tradition and Innovation

Rome was conscious of spreading its Roman civilization, but in each conquered territory it tried to absorb the traditions of the various peoples. The Romans took advantage of knowledge learned from other cultures to improve their own.

The Law

In the Greek polis, written law had marked a huge step forward in civilization, but law in the modern sense was created in Rome. Roman law still remains a lighthouse for the legal system of many modern countries.

Europe Inherits Rome

When the western Roman Empire started to crumble, lacking internal strength and finally dying away, the Roman civilization left to the European peoples the inheritance of its newest and most profound characteristics. One characteristic was its legal system, which was to blend with the customs of the various peoples, creating a new order. Another characteristic was the capacity of assimilation of other peoples and cultures. The Pax Deorum was another feature. It expressed the belief in an alliance with the gods.

SENATE
Originally it was formed of three hundred members elected for life. It dealt with foreign politics, war and military business, finances, taxes, and religion.

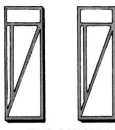

TWO CONSULS
For one year, they were the heads of the senate and of the comitia (assembly). They proposed new laws and were the commanders of the army.

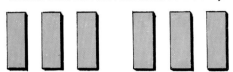

TWO TO EIGHT PRAETORS
(magistrates)
They were in charge for a year and conducted judicial inquiries.

DICTATOR
During a crisis, he would be appointed for a maximum of six months. He held all the power.

TWO CENSORS
They were in charge for five years. Their task was to register citizens on military, electoral, and tax lists. They watched over people's behavior and officially appointed the senators.

FOUR TO SIX AEDILES
They were in charge for one year and had control over the provisions of the city, the market, the public order, and entertainment.

FOUR TO FORTY QUAESTORS
They were in charge of finances for one year. They controlled all of the income.

TEN TRIBUNES OF THE PLEBEIANS
They were in charge for one year and could intervene in all issues. They could oppose the actions of the magistrates and the senate and oppose the proposed laws in the popular assemblies.

Comitia Curiata	**Comitia Centuriata**	**Comitia Tributa**
Originally, this was an assembly of shepherds and farmers. It retained its importance at all times and had the task of appointing the magistrates.	The participants were divided into classes according to their wealth, and each class was divided into centuries (groups), just like the army. They elected the consuls, the censors, and the praetors; decided upon peace or war; and judged the trials which involved capital punishment for Roman citizens.	The citizens of this assembly were divided into thirty-five rural and urban districts (called tribes) according to the place where they lived. Both patricians and plebeians had a right to vote. The assembly would elect aediles and quaestors, examine the body of laws, and act in judgement during trials of certain crimes.

PEOPLE'S ASSEMBLY

Everybody could participate in this assembly, but it was mainly attended by plebeians. The assembly elected the tribunes of the plebeians and the plebeian aediles. It would also vote on the laws, called plebiscites, proposed by the tribunes.

SOCIETY AND INSTITUTIONS IN REPUBLICAN ROME

Patricians, Nobles, and Knights

The patricians were the holders of political and religious strength. Besides them, another group of powerful people, the nobles, developed in Rome. They were the offspring of people who had held the most important magistratures. In as much as a public position would usually be passed from father to son, the class of the nobles had control over the main magistratures in Rome. The nobles were very wealthy. Their wealth was based on land. Life as a land-owner was considered the most dignified way of existence. Another class of very wealthy people was that of the knights who became numerous around the end of the Republican Age. They were plebeians (commoners) who had become rich and thus could hold public office. They could abandon activities which were considered undignified, such as commerce, and achieve a position comparable to that of the nobles. Eventually, they would incorporate into the noble class. These three classes—patricians, nobles, and knights—together never exceeded a few thousand people.

The Plebeians

Perhaps the class of Roman plebeians originated from conquered populations which migrated to Rome. In the Republican Age, the plebeians were not a homogenous group. They included poor peasants, who lived from their labor, and artisans and merchants, who were financially in a better position. In spite of these social and economic differences, the plebeian class was considered a unit by the state.

The Slaves

Like other civilizations in the ancient world but on a far greater scale, the Romans had slaves. Slaves were human beings who did not have any rights. In Rome, the slaves could be war prisoners, could be bought, or had become slaves because of debts. They were used in the most varied activities—for working in the mines, in the fields, on vast estates, or in specialized farming. Sometimes they would be installed as tenant farmers. In the city, domestic slaves worked in homes and sometimes would take care of the finances and help their masters in their artisan or trade activities. In some instances, the slaves would be released from servitude and obtain Roman citizenship.

At left: Shown is a chart of the magistratures of the republic.

The Client Relationship Between the Powerful and the Plebeians

Both patricians and nobles had their "clients" among the plebeians. They had the duty of welcoming the clients in their houses, feeding them when necessary, protecting them, and helping them. The clients had to give homage to the patrician or noble and back him in any public or private issue. The clients enjoyed the protection of the powerful, which was indispensable in political, legal, and economic life. The powerful, on the other hand, were all the more influential in town if they had a lot of clients.

The Base of Political Institutions in Rome

During the course of the centuries, the Roman public structure developed along with the growth of the city until a unit made of numerous magistratures and assemblies was created. The organization of power was based on the senate and on the people. In the Republican Age, the senate became the main political instrument. It dealt with foreign policy and war, checked finances and taxes, watched over religion, and watched over military affairs. The people expressed wishes through comitia or assemblies. These assemblies had political value, provided they met in accordance with the law. The comitia served the purpose of voting on the laws, handing down verdicts, and choosing the magistrates. The patricians and nobles controlled political life in Rome because they held the most important magistratures and because they organized voting procedures within the assembly.

The Plebeians Against Patricians and Nobles

Since the very beginning of the Republican Age, the plebeians, mainly the wealthiest among them, had claimed the right to partake in political decisions. In 494 B.C., the plebeians threatened to break the agreement which permitted the existence of the republic and withdrew from the sacred enclosure of the city. They returned to Rome only when they obtained their tribunes, an assembly of the plebeians, and some aediles.

The composition of Roman society is illustrated below.

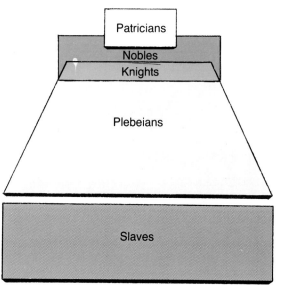

33

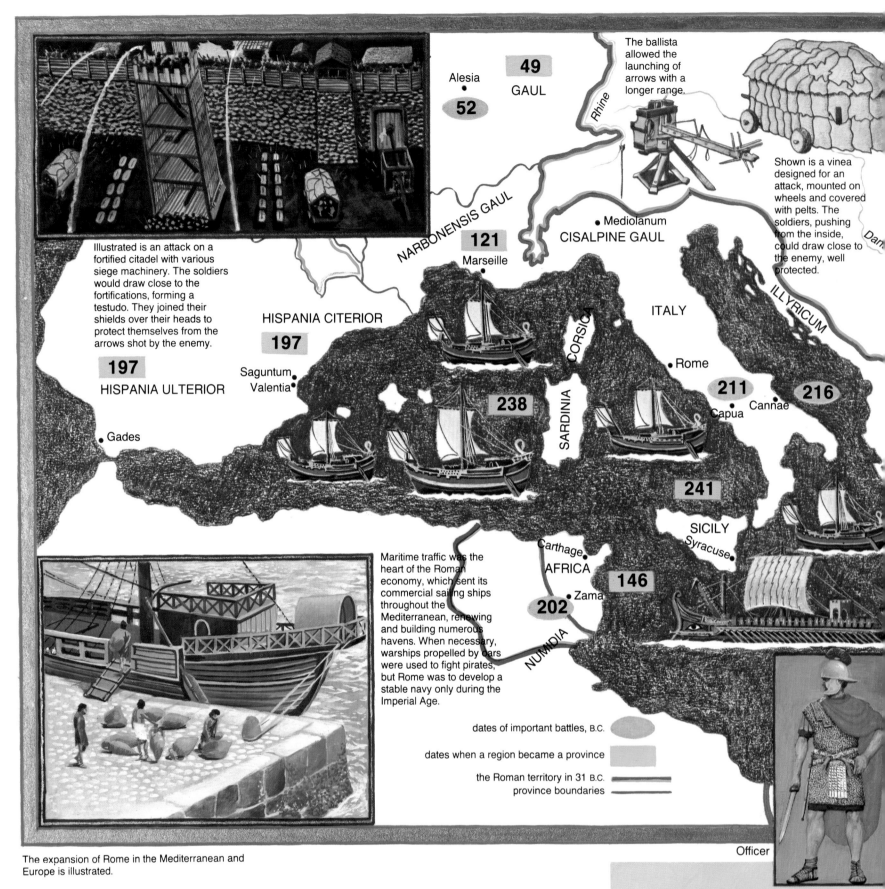

The ballista allowed the launching of arrows with a longer range.

Shown is a vinea designed for an attack, mounted on wheels and covered with pelts. The soldiers, pushing from the inside, could draw close to the enemy, well protected.

Illustrated is an attack on a fortified citadel with various siege machinery. The soldiers would draw close to the fortifications, forming a testudo. They joined their shields over their heads to protect themselves from the arrows shot by the enemy.

49 GAUL
Alesia
52

Rhine

NARBONENSIS GAUL
121 Marseille

CISALPINE GAUL
Mediolanum

ITALY
ILLYRICUM

HISPANIA CITERIOR
197
Saguntum
Valentia

CORSICA

Rome
211
Capua Cannae
216

HISPANIA ULTERIOR
197

SARDINIA
238

241

Gades

SICILY
Syracuse

Maritime traffic was the heart of the Roman economy, which sent its commercial sailing ships throughout the Mediterranean, renewing and building numerous havens. When necessary, warships propelled by oars were used to fight pirates, but Rome was to develop a stable navy only during the Imperial Age.

Carthage
AFRICA
Zama
146
202
NUMIDIA

dates of important battles, B.C.
dates when a region became a province
the Roman territory in 31 B.C.
province boundaries

Officer

The expansion of Rome in the Mediterranean and Europe is illustrated.

THE EXPANSION OF REPUBLICAN ROME

The First Steps

The Romans believed that they were destined by the gods to conquer others and demonstrated great skill in fostering the coexistence of diverse peoples. The young republic took its first steps in Italy against the Etruscan towns of the north, against the Latin allies, and against Greek towns in the south.

The Punic Wars

The Romans clashed with the Carthaginians in three wars for the dominion of the western half of the Mediterranean. As a result of the First Punic War (264-238 B.C.), the Romans gained Sardinia and Corsica. In the Second Punic War (221-202 B.C.) in spite of the victories of the Carthaginian General Hannibal in Italy, the

Arms and Strategy of the Roman Army

The Roman soldiers carried an oval or rectangular shield, a javelin, and a short sword. The strategic and tactical unit of the Roman army was the legion. Its four thousand members were divided into groups. Shown is a battle scheme from the third and second centuries. The velites formed a light infantry and attacked the enemy with bows and arrows and slingshots. The first line was composed of the lance hurlers. The

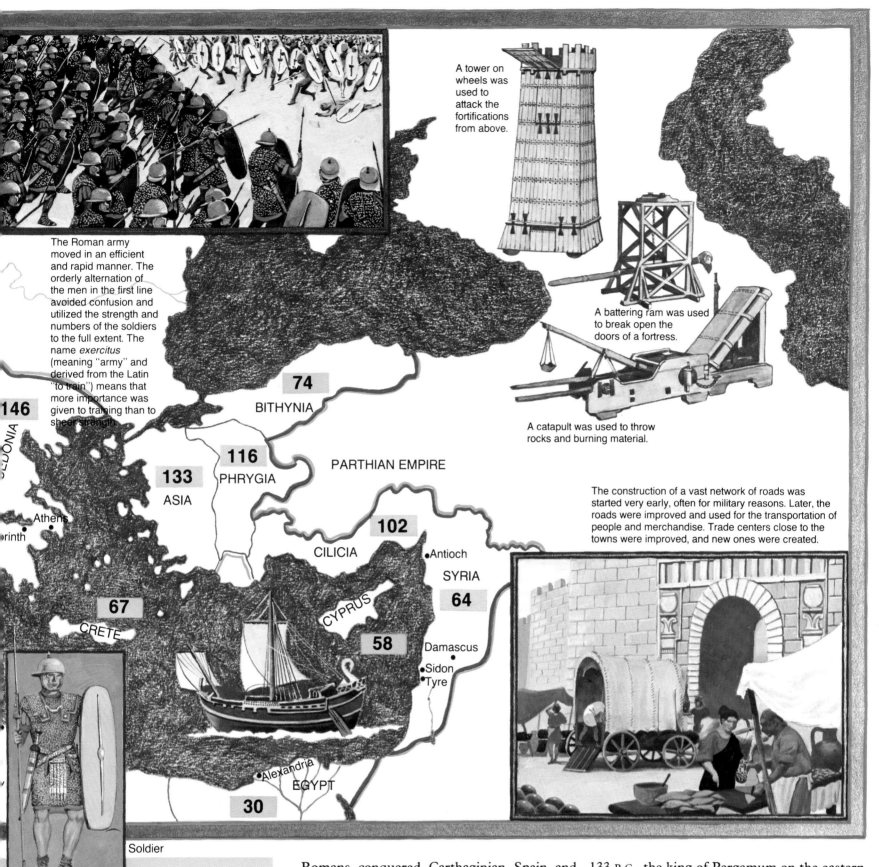

A tower on wheels was used to attack the fortifications from above.

A battering ram was used to break open the doors of a fortress.

A catapult was used to throw rocks and burning material.

The Roman army moved in an efficient and rapid manner. The orderly alternation of the men in the first line avoided confusion and utilized the strength and numbers of the soldiers to the full extent. The name *exercitus* (meaning "army" and derived from the Latin "to train") means that more importance was given to training than to sheer strength.

The construction of a vast network of roads was started very early, often for military reasons. Later, the roads were improved and used for the transportation of people and merchandise. Trade centers close to the towns were improved, and new ones were created.

146

MACEDONIA

Athens

Corinth

74

BITHYNIA

116

PHRYGIA

133

ASIA

PARTHIAN EMPIRE

102

CILICIA

•Antioch

SYRIA

CYPRUS

64

67

CRETE

58

Damascus

•Sidon
•Tyre

Soldier

Velites

Lance hurlers

Knights

Princeps

Triarii

•Alexandria

EGYPT

30

second line was composed of the most skilled men, the princeps. The third line was composed of triarii. The cavalry operated on the flanks.

Romans conquered Carthaginian Spain and later defeated the Carthaginians in Africa. In the Third Punic War (149-146 B.C.), the party which was in favor of expansion and colonization obtained a majority in Rome. As a result, Carthage was destroyed, and a Roman province in Africa was founded.

The Conquest of the East

At first, the Romans defended the independence of the Greek towns against the Hellenistic sovereigns, but later, in 148 B.C., Rome conquered Macedonia and Greece themselves. In

133 B.C., the king of Pergamum on the eastern shore of the Aegean Sea left his kingdom to the Romans, who turned it into a new province called Asia.

The Organization of the Provinces

In order to rule over populations with different cultures and political traditions, the Romans created new administrative units called the provinces, which were ruled by a Roman magistrate. The people of the provinces were not granted Roman citizenship.

The Celts manufactured iron tools for farming and artisanship, many of which are still in use today.

THE GAULS AND THE CELTIC WORLD

During the first centuries of the Roman republic, numerous tribes of Celtic populations had spread throughout the vast stretch of territory of temperate Europe from the Atlantic Ocean to the Black Sea. These peoples had created a civilization with a common language, culture, and religion. In the fourth century, some Celtic tribes reached the Italian peninsula and settled in the Po Valley and along the Adriatic coast to the south.

The Birth of the Oppidae

The Gauls, skilled farmers, had long been living in small villages, scattered about in the countryside, without gathering into more complex settlements. Around the third century, however, the tribes which lived in Cisalpine Gaul (the territory of the Po Valley) began to build fortified settlements of a primitive type, known by the Latin term *oppidum*. In the second century, several oppidae also existed in France, Germany, Bohemia, and Hungary.

The Oppidae, the First Towns of Temperate Europe

The Celtic oppidae were the first towns to

appear in Europe north of the Mediterranean region, which had already hosted urban civilizations for a considerable time. The oppidae were built on a rather large territory enclosed within sturdy defensive walls. The space within the wall was left partially free of buildings and used as a shelter for cattle as well as for farmers in case of danger. The towns possessed temples, aristocratic dwellings, homes, and artisan workshops.

Defense Fortifications

The existence of these towns reflected economic prosperity but also military uncertainty. Each town probably had a defense post. The protective walls were built of stone and lumber

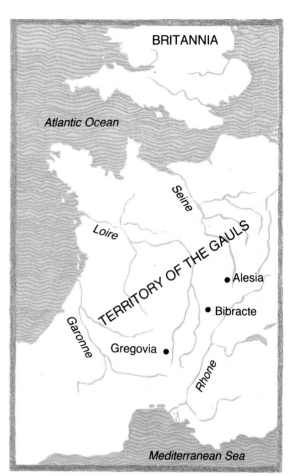

The map covers the territory of the Gauls, part of today's France, with the location of three important oppidae.

Shown is a view of a Celtic oppidum. The quarters for the artisans were located along the defensive walls, built using the "murus Gallicus" technique. Outside the town walls, wheat was harvested. The farmland shows a balance of woods, fields, and pastures. A priest, or druid, is shown returning from the woods where he gathered some magical herbs.

and invented the barrel, combining their knowledge of the working of iron and wood. They also worked with ceramics, glass, and enamels. Their great ability in working iron permitted them to manufacture all the tools they needed to perform various tasks. Tools of similar shape were found throughout Celtic Europe, which suggests that the general manufacturing techniques were known and used throughout the territory.

The Flourishing Countryside

The change which occurred in the countryside was less radical. In previous times, the Celts had already developed cultivation methods which allowed for the best use of the climatic and soil features of temperate Europe. Their extensive farming created the typical European landscape where fields alternated with pastures and woods. The improvement of artisan skills, however, gave agriculture more efficient iron tools, first and foremost the plowshare. The flourishing of agriculture made some Celtic regions, especially Gaul and Pannonia, particularly wealthy. These regions were more densely populated than others.

in the typical fashion which the Roman emperor Julius Caesar called "murus Gallicus." The walls reflected the influence of Mediterranean building techniques. These techniques were perhaps brought north of the Alps by Celts who had lived in the Mediterranean regions for some time. The fortified towns were a result of the presence of the Germans and, to the east along the Danube, the Dacians.

The Skilled Artisans of the Oppidae

The specialized artisans formed the most important and characteristic nucleus of the Celts of the oppidae. Their technical skills were outstanding. They were superb wagon-makers,

Shown is north-central Europe and the territory of the Germans.

Wooden shields found in a swamp in Denmark, dating back to around 100 B.C., are pictured.

THE GERMANS

At the end of the second century B.C., new tribes belonging to Germanic stock started to interact with the Roman and Celtic populations.

The Germans were a people composed of numerous tribes. They originated in the northern part of the European plain, in Denmark, and on the Scandinavian peninsula.

Celts and Germans

To the west and south, the Germanic territory bordered on Celtic territory. The two peoples had previously established commercial relationships, but the situation changed when the German tribes started to move toward the more desirable lands of central and southern Europe. The Germans had to face a somewhat

urbanized people who possessed a cavalry possibly organized into a permanent army. The strategies and fighting techniques of the two peoples were vastly different. Each Celt carried a long sword, a lance, and a shield. Celts wore helmets and were capable of attacking in formation. The Germans had a highly mobile light cavalry, which could rapidly draw close, launch its attack, and retreat.

The First Military Clash Between Celts and Romans

The Celtic people had long concluded their expansion. They had been defeated by the Romans, previously in Italy and more recently in Provence, on the southern coast of France.

There, in 125 B.C., the Romans founded the province of Narbonne Gaul. Around 120 B.C., a tribe coming from Denmark, the Cimbri, violently clashed with the most powerful Celtic tribe of central Europe, the Boii, which ruled over Bavaria. Following the route of amber, the Cimbri moved south and defeated the Romans in Styria (Austria). However, they did not march toward Italy but, within a few years, reached southern Gaul, together with other tribes of German and Celtic origin. The invaders stormed the region until they were defeated by the Romans in 102 B.C. at Aix-en-Provence and in 101 B.C. at Vercelli in the Po Valley.

Pressure from the German tribes continued, and several groups established settlements west

Shown is the typical hairstyle of a German, reconstructed on the basis of skulls found.

Depicted are houses in the German colony of Ezinge in Holland dating back to the third century B.C.

Shown is a votive bronze necklace in the shape of a crown from lower Saxony, Germany, third century B.C.

Above is a vase found in a cremation tomb in Denmark, dating back to the first century B.C.

Depicted is a cavalry clash between Gauls and Germans near Admagetobriga in the Alsace region. The Germans, led by Ariovistus, defeated the Gallic cavalry and settled on the lands of the Sequani Gauls. *Left inset:* a Gallic knight. *Right inset:* a German knight.

of the Rhine in northern Gaul. Around 70 B.C., the greatest pressure point was probably the region north of the Main River. The German leader Ariovistus, who lived in this region, was recruited with his army by the Sequani Gauls, who needed help in the battle against their arch rivals, the Aedui. In exchange for his services, Ariovistus obtained permission to settle in their territory, today's region of Alsace. Upon the arrival of the Germans, the Sequani, seized by panic, tried to resist them but were defeated at Admagetobriga on the Alsatian side of the Rhine. The domination of the Germans was so harsh that after a few years the Gauls asked for help from the Romans. The Romans, guided by Julius Caesar, defeated Ariovistus near Bresancon in 58 B.C. Caesar's plan was to establish the boundary of the German territory along the course of the Rhine so that he could easily control the territory of Gaul, which he was preparing to conquer. This plan was followed by all the other Roman emperors except for their short raids on the other side of the river. Neither the Gauls nor the Romans, however, succeeded in definitely chasing the Germans past the boundary of the Rhine, and they could not prevent other small groups from gradually infiltrating across the border and settling in the territory of Gaul.

Consequences of German Pressure on the Celtic World

The arrival of this new enemy caused serious problems for the Celts. In the same year of the defeat of Ariovistus, the Helvetians made an unsuccessful attempt at migrating west from their land in western Switzerland. They were stopped by other tribes and by the Romans, and had to return to the regions they had abandoned. Their population was almost cut in half. At the end of the first century B.C., the German tribe of Marcomanni, led by Maroboduus, reached the territory of the Boians in central Europe. The Quadi tribe invaded today's Moravia, more to the east. The Celtic culture which flourished in these territories was crushed within a short time. Numerous oppidae were destroyed, part of the population fled the country, and part was conquered by these newcomers.

Marius (155-86 B.C.)

Sulla (138-78 B.C.)

Pompey (106-48 B.C.)

Crassus (115-53 B.C.)

Julius Caesar
(100-44 B.C.)

In the first decades of the first century B.C., a major economic crisis swept Rome, causing a number of riots. This drawing shows a mob looting a bakery.

THE CRISIS OF THE REPUBLIC AND JULIUS CAESAR

The Defense of Vast Properties in the Countryside

Early Roman economy was based on raising livestock and farming small plots. The land was worked by the entire family with the help of a few slaves. When the small landowners began to serve as soldiers in the many battles fought by Rome, they sometimes had to abandon their land. The inexpensive importation of wheat from the provinces caused the decline of the traditional Italian grain cultivation. Patricians introduced vineyards, olive groves, vegetables, and fruit trees. These new crops often required intensive labor and high expense. Thus, the small farmers had to sell their plots. This reduced the number of free landowners. Senators and knights who had the political power and the economic means could take advantage of the land seizures. In this way, medium and large estates were created.

Rome's Wealth Increases

Great riches in currency and gold, principally the booty of war, began to flow into Rome. Moreover, the systematic exploitation of the provinces provided large quantities of money both to the state and to private enterprises. The population of Rome increased greatly, due also to the migration of impoverished people from the countryside. Urban development and public works multiplied the opportunities for work and circulated the great wealth. In 269 B.C., Rome started to mint silver coins.

The Political and Social Struggle

Starting in the second half of the second century, these changes caused several kinds of political and social crises in which nobles, plebeians, and slaves were at odds. There were attempts to take illegally held grazing land away

from the great livestock farmers and divide the land among the citizens. In 104-102 B.C., the slaves of Campania and Sicily rebelled. In 72-71 B.C., Spartacus led a war between the abused slaves and Rome. The riots were harshly repressed. In 91 B.C., the confederate Italics started a war which was concluded with their attainment of citizenship in 89 B.C. Soon, an economic crisis burst upon Rome. The city was overcrowded with refugees, provisions were scarce, and prices were inflating. Riots broke out in which there were two adversary factions. The senate and the nobles wished their power and privilege to remain unchanged. But the wealthy plebeians, called populares, wanted to attain political power equal to their economic power, plus they wanted decisive action in foreign affairs including attempts at colonization. Marius was the leader of the popular movement, while Sulla was backed by most of the

Roman soldiers confiscate lands in a Gallic village they have just conquered and are chasing away the former inhabitants.

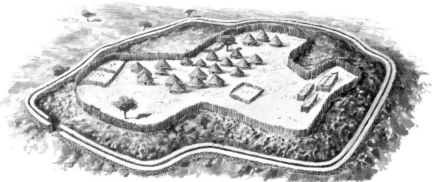

Reconstruction of the Celtic oppidum of Bigbury in England is shown. It was similar to the ones Caesar found during his raid in 55 B.C.

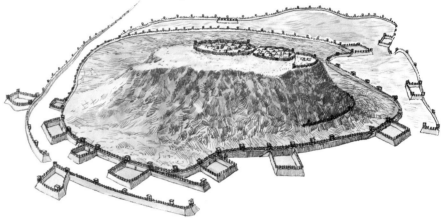

Pictured is the site of the Battle of Alesia. On top of the hill, there was a fortified Gallic oppidum surrounded by a double line of siege fortifications which the Romans had built to cut off supplies.

The triumph of a commander

FORUM JULIUM

The Forum of Julius Caesar

The forum was a central square surrounded by temples, public buildings, colonnades, and stores, with statues, inscriptions, and commemorative columns. It was the financial, religious, and administrative center of the city. Julius Caesar also created a new square with a temple dedicated to Venus Genetrix to give thanks for the victory over Pompey.

nobles and the wealthiest classes. Sulla prevailed and violently imposed his dictatorship in Rome for three years.

The Ascent of Caesar

Several years of internal conflict followed. Among the most famous struggles for power and the ensuing conspiracies was the conspiracy of Catiline.

Caius Julius Caesar, belonging to a noble Roman family, partook in the conspiracy and sided with Catiline against the aristocratic proconsul Cicero. When the conspiracy failed, Caesar left Rome for some years. In 60 B.C., he returned and founded an informal alliance, the first triumvirate. He was assigned to the rule of Cisalpine Gaul and Narbonensis Gaul for five years. In 58 B.C., he went to the provinces that had been assigned to him and began the conquest of the rest of the Gallic lands. He clashed with the courageous king Vercingetorix of the Arverni, who created serious problems for Caesar's legions. The decisive battle occurred around the oppidum of Alesia, where Vercingetorix had sought shelter. After a long siege, Caesar forced the enemy to surrender and in 51 B.C., made Gaul into a Roman province. Due to the victories attained in Gaul, Caesar could return to Rome victorious and impose his will on the senate. After defeating his rival Pompey, he gained indisputable political dominion over the state.

Toward the Empire

With Caesar, the eastern concept of a universal sovereign started to take hold in Rome. In 44 B.C., Caesar was assassinated by about sixty senators who were the last defenders of the republic.

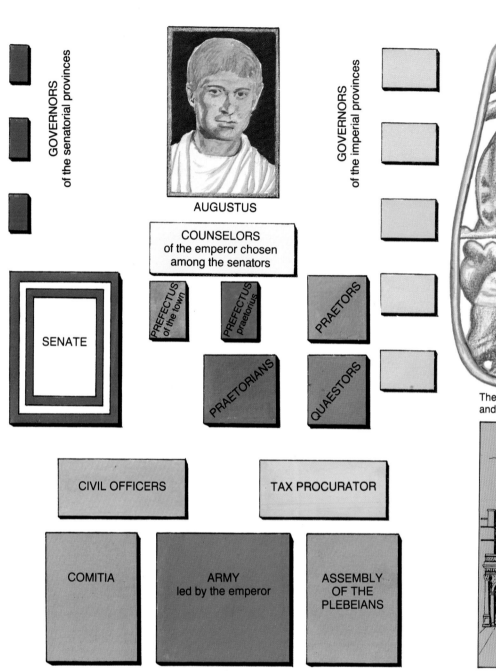

GOVERNORS
of the senatorial provinces

AUGUSTUS

GOVERNORS
of the imperial provinces

COUNSELORS
of the emperor chosen
among the senators

PREFECTUS
of the town

PREFECTUS
praetorius

PRAETORS

SENATE

PRAETORIANS

QUAESTORS

CIVIL OFFICERS

TAX PROCURATOR

COMITIA

ARMY
led by the emperor

ASSEMBLY
OF THE
PLEBEIANS

Octavian Augustus was at the center of the political
organization of the principate.

The jewel of Augustus shows the emperor with the goddess Rome *(upper)*
and Roman soldiers putting a statue in place *(lower)*.

Illustrated is the forum erected by Augustus with the temple
dedicated to Mars the Avenger.

THE BIRTH OF THE EMPIRE:
THE PRINCIPATE OF OCTAVIAN AUGUSTUS

The Rise of Octavian

After the death of Caesar, the struggle for power in Rome resumed. The second triumvirate was created. Each triumvirate had a sphere of influence. Octavian ruled over the west, Lepidus ruled over Africa, and Mark Antony ruled over the east. But this division of power was not to last long, and soon Octavian started off on his conquest of the Roman state. He violently expelled the senate and the friends of Antony. In 31 B.C. in the battle of Actium, he defeated Antony's fleet, which was backed by the Egyptian fleet of Cleopatra. Lepidus had already retired from political life. So after the defeat of Antony, Octavian became the uncontested ruler of Rome's empire.

The Principate

Octavian considered himself the supreme defender of Rome and its tradition, in contrast to the model of the eastern monarchies. After his victory, he devised an original way of imposing his power, while preserving the traditional political institutions. This type of government was called a principate. Octavian laid the foundation for the principate upon collaboration with the major powers of Roman society. He didn't embark upon sudden and major reform of the political institutions but rather reformed them gradually, continually concentrating more power in his own hands. He respected the authority of the senate and didn't modify its constitution but appointed himself president of the senate.

He took the power of the tribunes of the plebeians for himself and kept the position permanently, rather than for one year. His authority, his moral influence, his personal dignity, together with his military expertise made him, in fact, superior to anyone else. In 27 B.C. in recognition of his authority, he was given the title of "Augustus," which acknowledged his position of great prestige and the fact that he was protected by the gods. Later, in 12 B.C., Octavian obtained the position of "pontifex maximus" which made him the head of the Roman priests.

Octavian Augustus divided the provinces into two groups—imperial and senatorial. The former was directly administered by him through trusted legates, while the latter was under the

The Roman army is shown attacking an Alpine fortification. The conquering of the Alps and the creation of new provinces in these regions was one of the main successes of Augustus. *To the left* is the giant monument of the Turbie, built in Provence in 7-6 B.C. It honored the conquering of the Alpine tribes between 16 and 14 B.C.

charge of the representatives of the senate.

Taxes from the senate-controlled provinces were collected in the treasury of the state. Taxes coming from the imperial provinces were collected in the personal treasury of the emperor, for the personal benefit of Octavian Augustus. The new organization of the provinces provided some relief for the local populations because it markedly reduced the abuse of power that had occurred during the Republican Age. Moreover, the provinces had the power to directly appeal to the emperor in case of discontent.

Military Campaigns

The principal aims of Augustus were the pacification of the land which had already been annexed to the empire, together with the creation of a stable border. His main concern was conquering the tribes of the Alpine people, who still retained their independence. He succeeded in imposing Roman domination and creating new provinces. To the north, the Romans invaded German territories and tried to expand all the way to Elba Island, but they were driven back by the Germans under the leadership of the prince of the Cherusci, Arminius, who had served in the Roman army. The battle occurred in the woods of Teutoberg in 9 B.C. The Roman border was consolidated along the Rhine. To the east, Augustus had to give up the plan of imposing his military dominion over the kingdoms of the Parthians and of the Armenians.

THE ROMAN RELIGION

The Roman Olympus

The Roman Olympus, which was the group of gods worshipped by Roman people, was originally composed of a triad of deities—Jupiter, the god who had supreme sovereignty; Mars, the god of war; and Quirinus, the god of the city. During the period of the monarchy, due to influence from the Etruscans, great importance had been given to Juno and Minerva. The former was the wife of Jupiter and the goddess of fertility; the latter was the protectress of all professions.

The Alliance with the Gods

The Romans believed in the Pax Deorum (the peace with the gods) and considered it an absolute necessity. It was an alliance between the gods and all Roman citizens. The feeling was that Rome would endure because the gods were by its side. The Greeks felt helpless in the face of death, which put an end to any creation and development. The Romans, on the other hand, forged a connection between the dead and the living through their sense of great unity with their ancestors.

Priests

The numerous groups of priests had the task of celebrating the rituals of the main deities. The principal holders of the sacred sciences were called the pontifex. They knew the calendar, the most suitable invocations and prayers, and the rules which regulated the various temples. They formed a college guided by the pontifex maximus. In Rome, special importance was given to Vesta, the goddess who guaranteed the continuous existence of the city. A perpetual flame burned in the middle of a small round temple, dedicated to Vesta. Should the flame go out, Rome would be destroyed. Some special priestesses who could never marry called Vestal Virgins dedicated their lives exclusively to the goddess and the preservation of the fire.

Family Pietas and the Domestic Cult

The roots of Roman religion rested within the life of each home and family. Obedience to one's father, called family pietas, was the foundation of Roman civilization.

Precise rituals accompanied the major steps in a Roman's life—birth, adolescence, marriage, and death. Marriage, for example, took place under the protection of Juno and of the household deities. In ancient times, there was always a fire burning at the center of the house,

1. SOME OF THE ROMAN GODS

2. FAMILY CULT

3. FAMILY PIETAS

4. CULT OF VESTA

5. THE IMPERIAL CULT

6. THE PUBLIC SACRIFICE

7. A WEDDING

8. THE CULT OF ISIS

later replaced by an altar located in the communal room. Among the offerings were flower garlands, incense, wine, honey, and sweets.

The Cult of the Emperor

Augustus had given Rome peace, freeing it from the threat of internal strife and consolidating Roman power in the world. Thus, it was not difficult for the Romans to consider such a man to be divine. The divinity of Augustus was honored both in Rome and in the provinces. After him, the deification of the emperors became the rule. The senate had the task of declaring the divinity of the emperor after his death, and all the inhabitants of the empire were expected to celebrate the imperial cult. Whoever did not follow this rule would endanger the solidity of the empire itself and its continuation.

The Crisis of Roman Religion and Religious Influence from the East

After the Punic Wars and during the internal fights of the Republican Age, the Romans started to realize that perhaps they couldn't totally trust the alliance with the gods, who did not seem to provide an answer for the doubts and sufferings of people. The concept of a relationship between human beings and their destiny was starting to develop. What would have happened after the fall of Rome? The great power of Rome itself was no longer sufficient to give meaning to human life and death. Thus, different explanations were sought in the east. In the first century B.C., the cult of Isis was introduced from Egypt. In this cult, a few chosen individuals would perform rituals representing death, followed by resurrection.

1) Jupiter, Juno, Minerva, and Mars. **2)** In the atrium of the house, in front of the altar of the Lares, the head of the family is about to celebrate a ritual. **3)** The son must completely obey his father in reference to the ancient tradition. The walnut was the symbol of youth as was the bulla, which youths wore around their necks until they were seventeen years of age. **4)** Priestesses head to the temple of Vesta, where the eternal flame, representing the goddess, burns. **5)** The praetorians give homage to the imperial deity, saluting the emperor with their arms outstretched. **6)** In front of each temple is an altar where sacrifices to the gods are made. **7)** The wedding celebration is rich in symbols. The bride must wear a special dress and a veil. When she reaches the house of the groom, she can't touch the threshold but has to be carried through it by her friends. She wears a ring on her ring finger, which according to the Romans, contains a nerve that runs all the way to the heart. **8)** A priest is celebrating a sacrifice on an Egyptian-style altar. Another priest is descending the staircase. He carries a vase possibly containing water from the Nile.

Daily Life in Imperial Rome

Rome, Capital of an Empire

The situation in Rome was changing. Rome was no longer the city of the early Republican Age, where the people had a life-style similar to that of herdsmen and farmers of the countryside. The city was powerful. It was the meeting place for people from distant provinces, and a great deal of wealth circulated there. Its population was large, and at the time of Augustus, it reached about one million. Life in Rome offered the best and the worst of urban experience in ancient times. On the one hand, it allowed for communication between people and the exchange of customs, varied languages, and religions. On the other hand, the large Roman population did not have a stable source of income and was fond of violent entertainment such as gladiator events where men had to kill each other.

The Construction of Large Apartment Buildings

In order to house an increasingly large population, the Romans devised a special kind of housing called the insula. It was a building comprised of several apartments similar to modern condominiums. The insula could be as tall as five or six stories and soon became the most popular kind of housing in the city. Buildings of this kind were found both in Rome and Ostia, a densely-populated harbor town at the outlet of the Tiber. The city of Rome did not have rich sections and poor sections. On the contrary, the houses of the nobles and the insula intermingled.

On the right is an aerial view of the Trajan market, a large commercial center with shops placed on several levels. This complex was part of the new grandiose forum which Trajan erected on the side of the forum of Augustus in the center of Rome.

Below is how the shops lined along a Roman street looked. Shown is a blacksmith's shop, a poultry shop, a money lender, a grocery store, and a shop selling ready-to-eat food. In the background is an insula, a typical apartment building built on several levels.

DWELLINGS OF THE NOBLES IN THE CITY AND THE COUNTRYSIDE

In the city, the nobles lived with their families in the domus, an individually owned house. The house stretched out longitudinally and was richly appointed with furniture, statues, and frescoes.

Usually, nobles owned several villas in the country. These were large farmhouses located

An inspector examines the construction of some vases.

in the center of property where labor was organized, cattle took shelter, and produce could be stored and processed. Part of the building was used as a dwelling by the owner, who lived there from time to time. The farming activities were under the direction of an administrator who organized the labor of the numerous slaves. These types of villas were to become widespread throughout the countryside.

POLIBIVS

18

1

2

3

3

Pictured is a reconstruction of the villa of Boscoreale in southern Italy. In the second inner courtyard are vases partially buried in the ground, which were used to store produce.

The rooms of the Domus
1. Entrance or "fauces"
2. Atrium, originally the site of the eternal flame and later the central part of the public section of the house
3. Servant's room
4. Office of owner or of his administrative slave
5. Living room or "tablinium"
6. Hallway
7. Bathroom

Inside the atrium of a noble's domus, three clients wait for the owner to appear. In the kitchen (9), a slave is working, and in the weaving room (17), another slave is unrolling a carpet which she has taken off the loom.

8. Inner courtyard with garden
9. Kitchen
10. Storage room
11. Oven
12. Bath "calidarium"
13. Bath "tepidarium"
14. Bath "apoditerium"
15. Summer "triclinium"
16. Bedroom
17. Weaving room
18. The library and dining room are in this section of the atrium.

A noble has his marble bust sculpted. The cabinet in the background contains the busts of some ancestors. These figures were carried in a procession on the occasion of the funeral of a family member, and the right to own and use them was a privilege reserved for the noble class. The nobility of the family was measured by the number of the images which were preserved in the domus.

Pictured is a cross section of the Pantheon, a temple built by Hadrian in A.D. 126. It is composed of a portico connected to a circular room which is covered by a large, exquisitely designed dome.

Below is a frieze from the Column of Trajan depicting the emperor attacking the barbarians.

Below is another frieze from the Column of Trajan showing the triumph of the emperor, while the defeated enemies are asking for mercy.

Poetry readings were held in the library of Maecenas in Rome.

In the middle left is the Column of Trajan erected in Rome by Trajan in A.D. 113 to celebrate his conquests. It is decorated with a magnificent marble frieze which winds all the way from the base to the top.

THE POET VIRGIL

LAW, ART, AND LITERATURE OF THE EMPIRE

Law and a Legal System Develop in Rome

The Romans developed the idea that the political interactions between people should be regulated by a system of laws. In the beginning, Roman law was composed of religious rituals and of rules that were handed down, which only applied to Roman born individuals. However, as the republic expanded, new regulations had to be introduced which were also applicable to nonnative Romans. In fact, relationships with nonnatives were becoming more and more frequent. The Roman lawmakers then began to elaborate on the idea of a system of justice which was uniform for all people, regardless of differences in citizenship, class, or wealth. In the first century B.C., the Romans proclaimed the existence of a natural law which stated that all people were equal. This concept was voiced by Cicero, a famous lawmaker and politician. In short, the law of the state was only partially the result of laws issued in the assemblies. Many of the regulations could be drawn in a judicial process, and the controversial issues could be solved following the natural principles of justice and equity. The state's law was above everything, and the magistrates drew their authority from it. In the words of Cicero, in order to be free, an individual had to obey the law.

Literature and Poetry Reached the Height of Expression

Under the dominion of Augustus, culture flourished in Rome. Many poets and writers would gather in the city house or country villa of Maecenas, the faithful collaborator of Augustus. The emperor himself followed their activities, which were supposed to celebrate the peace

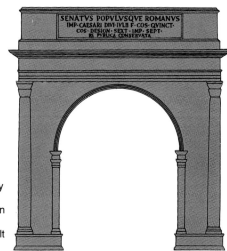

Two examples of arches are shown. To the right is an early arch in honor of Augustus erected in the Roman forum in 29 B.C. Below is a later arch also in honor of Augustus built in the forum around 20 B.C.

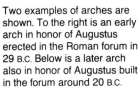

THE POET HORACE

Pictured is a magistrate wearing a toga edged in purple. He holds the scroll of the law, which indicates that he is invested with judicial authority. In the background is part of the text of a law carved in bronze.

and power of Rome. Among the scholars of this circle were Horace, the poet who sang with wonderful expression of personal experiences and daily events, and Virgil, who sang about the revived interest in agriculture.

The Development of Imperial Art

The influence of Greek and Hellenistic art was still seen in Roman art at the time of Augustus. In his funeral monument the *Ara Pacis* in bas-relief, Augustus left a great testimony to how the models of Athens and Pergamus influenced Roman art. All the monuments of Augustus were based on the idea that artistic expression must exalt the emperor and the grandeur of Rome. This tendency was to develop greatly in the first century A.D. when it was commonly accepted that buildings, sculptures, and bas-reliefs should express the idea of the power and stability of the empire. The grandeur of Rome can also be seen in the imposing size of public works. With respect to their beauty, the bridges, aqueducts, city gates, forums, and amphitheaters of the Imperial Age are among the best artworks of ancient times.

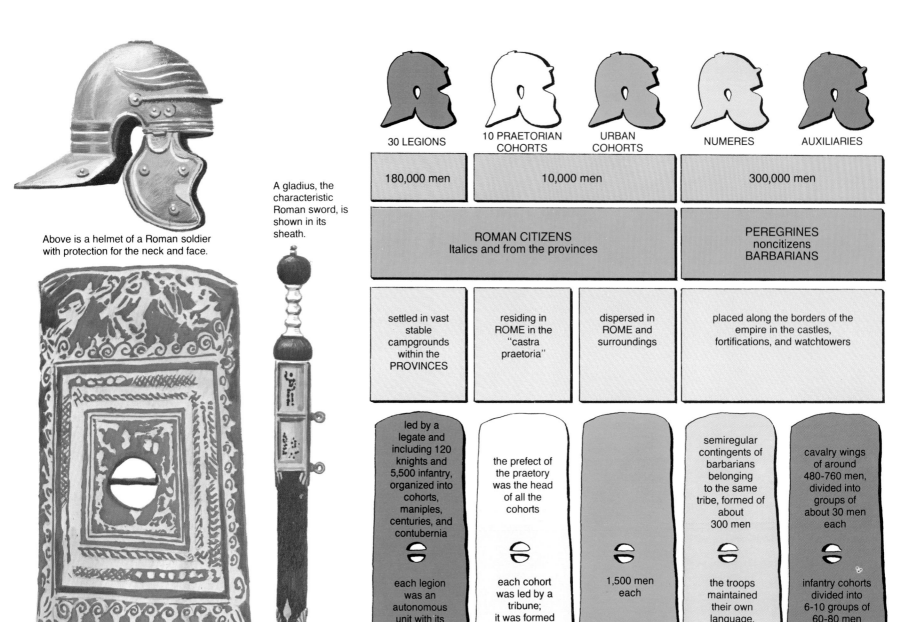

Above is a helmet of a Roman soldier with protection for the neck and face.

A gladius, the characteristic Roman sword, is shown in its sheath.

Pictured is a tile shield of a legionary.

30 LEGIONS	10 PRAETORIAN COHORTS	URBAN COHORTS	NUMERES	AUXILIARIES
180,000 men	10,000 men		300,000 men	
ROMAN CITIZENS Italics and from the provinces			PEREGRINES noncitizens BARBARIANS	
settled in vast stable campgrounds within the PROVINCES	residing in ROME in the "castra praetoria"	dispersed in ROME and surroundings	placed along the borders of the empire in the castles, fortifications, and watchtowers	
led by a legate and including 120 knights and 5,500 infantry, organized into cohorts, maniples, centuries, and contubernia	the prefect of the praetory was the head of all the cohorts		semiregular contingents of barbarians belonging to the same tribe, formed of about 300 men	cavalry wings of around 480-760 men, divided into groups of about 30 men each
each legion was an autonomous unit with its technical engineers, provisions, and pack animals	each cohort was led by a tribune; it was formed of 90 knights and 500 infantry	1,500 men each	the troops maintained their own language, arms, equipment, and fighting techniques	infantry cohorts divided into 6-10 groups of 60-80 men each, then divided into groups of 8 men each

THE STRUCTURE OF THE ROMAN ARMY

THE PAX ROMANA

A Peace Which Lasted Two Centuries

The rule of Augustus ushered in a period of exceptional economic, social, and political well-being within the Roman Empire. The two centuries of peaceful existence and social development which followed were unique and remained unequaled in all of Roman history.

Emperors of the Principate

The model established by Augustus, which resulted in the union of emperor and nobles, army and senate, capital and provinces, gave political tranquility to the empire throughout the Principate period. Augustus did not have any offspring but adopted Tiberius, who after the death of Augustus in A.D. 14, ruled the empire and founded the Julius-Claudian dynasty. This dynasty ended with the death of Nero in A.D. 68. After a brief period of war between competing Roman armies, Vespasianus took power, founding the Flavian dynasty. Upon the death of Domitianus in 96, the senate claimed for itself the right to appoint new emperors. This move allowed for the continuation of the fruitful alliance between emperors and the noble class and put at the head of the Roman empire men who were endowed with high political and moral qualities. These men were not necessarily Roman born. The Antonine emperors, chosen by the senate, were the best in Roman history. Under Trajan and Hadrian, the empire reached by conquest its maximum expanse.

A Cosmopolitan Empire

Rome felt invested with a political and cultural mission toward the people of the Mediterranean and Europe. The enterprise of unifying all of the civil world under a sole dominion was successful because Rome did not dominate in an absolute way. On the contrary, it permitted the coexistence of the diverse cultures which intermingled within the great cosmopolitan empire. It also permitted those who resisted conquest to die in battle or be enslaved.

Participation in Politics

The Romans conceded varying degrees of participation in the political life of the empire to the conquered people. When a group of Roman citizens settled in a certain site on conquered

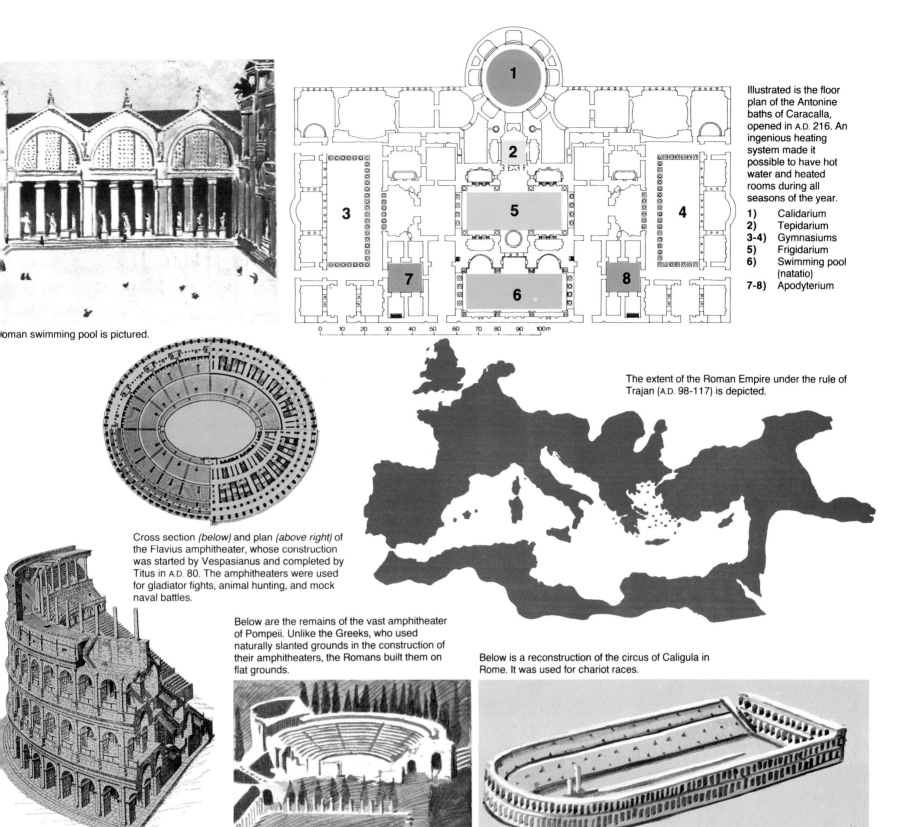

Roman swimming pool is pictured.

Illustrated is the floor plan of the Antonine baths of Caracalla, opened in A.D. 216. An ingenious heating system made it possible to have hot water and heated rooms during all seasons of the year.

1) Calidarium
2) Tepidarium
3-4) Gymnasiums
5) Frigidarium
6) Swimming pool (natatio)
7-8) Apodyterium

Cross section (below) and plan (above right) of the Flavius amphitheater, whose construction was started by Vespasianus and completed by Titus in A.D. 80. The amphitheaters were used for gladiator fights, animal hunting, and mock naval battles.

The extent of the Roman Empire under the rule of Trajan (A.D. 98-117) is depicted.

Below are the remains of the vast amphitheater of Pompeii. Unlike the Greeks, who used naturally slanted grounds in the construction of their amphitheaters, the Romans built them on flat grounds.

Below is a reconstruction of the circus of Caligula in Rome. It was used for chariot races.

and, a colony was created giving the new citizens Roman citizenship with full political rights. When, on the other hand, the Romans encountered an urban settlement of a certain sophistication, they let it be ruled by its own magistrates and with its own rules, and established a civitas. The inhabitants of the civitas did not have Roman citizenship. If a town were surrounded by a markedly Romanized territory, it would become a municipium. The inhabitants of the municipiae did not have the right to vote.

The Army, the Means of Construction of the Empire

The military establishment contributed to the creation of the empire. The army was the point of contact for exchange of varied customs and Roman values.

Roman citizens, immigrants from the provinces, and barbarians from the borders served in the army under the command of Roman civilians, nobles, and knights. In the Imperial Age, the army was reorganized by Augustus himself.

The emperor, in his effort to provide Rome with a permanent and skilled army, had based the military establishment on two pillars—the legions, which included all the Roman citizens and the Romanized peoples, and the auxilia, formed of other conquered peoples of the empire or of barbarians. At the end of the second century A.D., the Roman army numbered about 500,000.

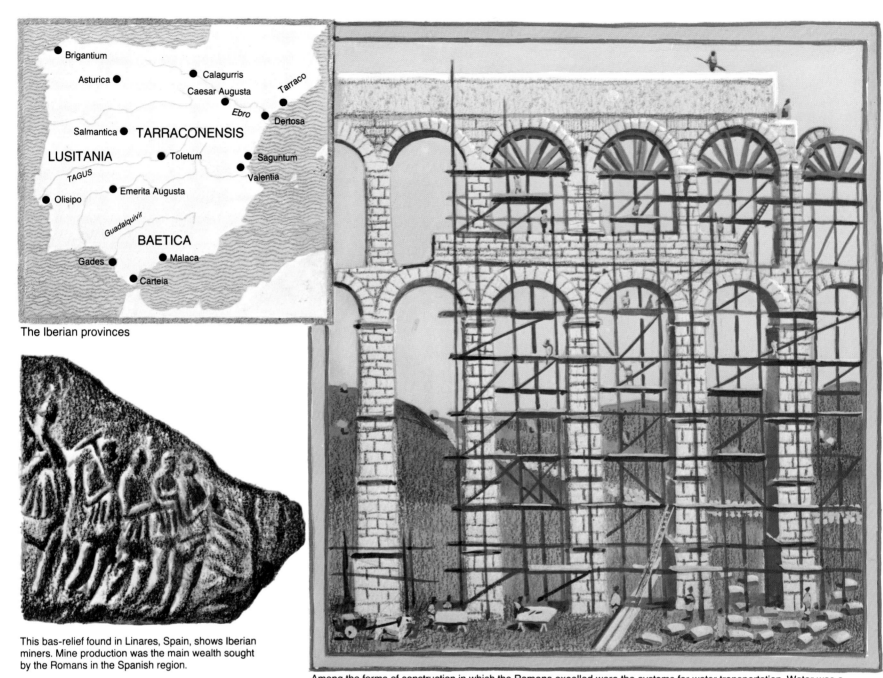

The Iberian provinces

This bas-relief found in Linares, Spain, shows Iberian miners. Mine production was the main wealth sought by the Romans in the Spanish region.

Among the forms of construction in which the Romans excelled were the systems for water transportation. Water was a necessity for both farming and urban life. The illustration shows the construction of a double level aqueduct in a Spanish valley. Water would flow inside a conduit placed over the second row of arches.

THE PROVINCES OF SPAIN AND GAUL

Spain was the first large western region to fall under Roman dominion during the Punic Wars. Prior to the Roman conquest, Iberian, Greek, Carthaginian, and Celtic-Iberian populations lived on the Iberian Peninsula. They were politically organized and grouped in various ways, extending from true cities and commercial centers to tribes of farmers and shepherds. Spain, under Roman administration, was divided into three regions—Baetica, Lusitania, and Tarraconensis.

The Economy of the Iberian Provinces

The principal economic riches of Spain came from gold, silver, tin, lead, copper, iron, and mercury mines. After the depletion of the Greek mines, Spain had become the main sup-plier of precious and common metals, which were used throughout the empire. The plentiful production of wheat, oil, and wine made a sizable contribution to the provisions of Rome and Italy as well as Spain. Following in Rome's tradition of great military skill, Spain provided a reserve of infantry and knights for the Roman army. The process of the Romanization in Spain was especially intensive along the Mediterranean, while the northern population put up strong resistance to a brutal conquest, then to the use of Latin and to the practice of the official Roman religion.

Society and Culture

The Roman administration built numerous towns in Spain. At the beginning, they were mainly colonies which were interconnected by a vast network of roads. Major aqueduct systems were built with slave labor to assure the continual supply of fresh water. Aqueducts and dams are among the most famous Roman monuments still in existence today. Particularly in the first century, Spain contributed greatly to Roman culture. The most important Latin writers of the time were from Spain. Among them were the philosopher Seneca, the poets Lucanian and Martial, and the orator Quintilianus. Spain even gave Rome two emperors, Trajan and Hadrian.

The Gauls

Prior to Roman conquest, some Greek settlements dotted the Mediterranean coast of Gaul. The rest of the territory was divided among numerous peoples and Celtic tribes. The con-

A Gallic-Roman lord welcomes a guest in the yard in front of his villa. Gallics willingly accepted the Roman way of thinking and behaving.

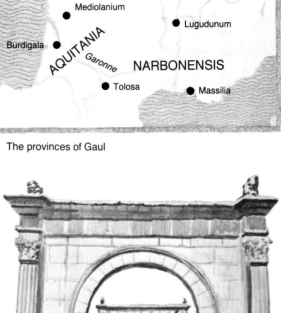

The provinces of Gaul

When the Romans built a provincial town, they often erected a gateway decorated with arches, which commemorated the founding of the town. Shown are the arches of St. Remy in Provence built at the time of Augustus.

quest occurred in several phases. First the southern part of Gaul was conquered, creating the province of Narbonensis Gaul. Later, the central and northern part was conquered and became the provinces of Aquitania, Lugdunensis Gaul, and Belgica Gaul. Narbonensis Gaul was the province that was Romanized most quickly, and the number of Roman towns within it multiplied greatly. The process of Romanization of the other provinces included the construction of towns on the sites of the oppidae which had been the capitals of the different tribes. These towns attained the status of civitas. Each civitas had control over a vast territory in accordance with the Celtic tradition which maintained a relationship between the tribal center and the surrounding countryside.

The Development of the Economy

Gaul increased its agricultural resources, which were wheat, barley, wine, oil, fruit, and vegetables. Many of these products were exported, creating problems of competition with other producing nations. The wine of the Gauls, for example, soon entered into competition with wine from Italy, which was traditionally backed by the Roman government. During the course of this wine battle, the emperors enacted a series of restrictive regulations on vineyards in Gaul. Artisan activity was widespread in Gaul, and in some cases it represented minor industries which used labor outside of the family of the owner. This was the case, for example, in the making of glass and ceramics which replaced, on western markets, production from Italy.

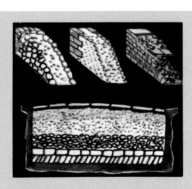

There were three Roman techniques used to build walls *(left to right)*—irregular bricks (opus incertum), diagonally placed bricks (opus reticulatum), and triangular blocks (opus testaceum). Shown below is the construction technique for a Roman road. In this cross section are the different layers of materials which were used to insure solidity and water drainage. The surface layer was made of stone slabs that were resistant to wear from traffic.

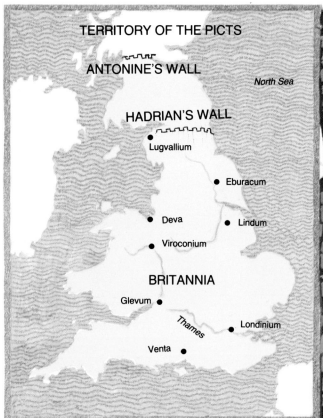

TERRITORY OF THE PICTS

ANTONINE'S WALL

North Sea

HADRIAN'S WALL

Lugvallium

Eburacum

Deva   Lindum

Viroconium

BRITANNIA

Glevum

Thames   Londinium

Venta

The provinces of Britannia

The wall of Hadrian, named in honor of the emperor, was a defensive fortification against the populations of the northern regions. It was made with stones and tufa and followed the contours of the hills. It was furnished with watchtowers and forts and was regularly patrolled by troops.

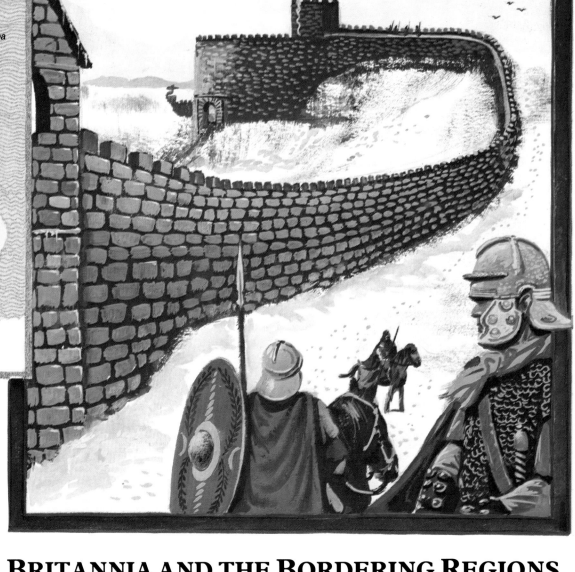

This burial stone from the second century A.D. shows a blacksmith pounding an anvil.

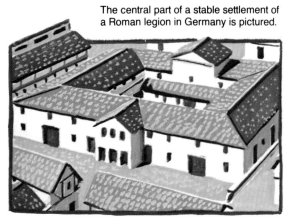

The central part of a stable settlement of a Roman legion in Germany is pictured.

BRITANNIA AND THE BORDERING REGIONS ALONG THE RHINE

The Conquest of Britannia

Britannia, at the beginning of its conquest by Rome in 43 B.C., was inhabited by a Celtic population and was divided into chiefdoms. These chiefdoms offered strenuous resistance to the Romans for many years. The Romans could never gain control over all the islands. Caledonia, with the advantage of its mountainous terrain corresponding to modern Scotland, always eluded conquest. Hadrian, after A.D. 122, built a fortified wall to mark the limes. After A.D. 140 during the age of the Antonines, the Roman army pushed further on, and a new wall was built more to the north. Past this wall was the territory of the unconquered Picts.

Roman Towns in Britannia

The majority of the tribal centers in Britannia were built on hills and were well protected. According to the Romans, these were not the best sites for a town, which they considered the center of communication for military, commer-cial, and administrative purposes. For this reason, Rome independently founded its network of fortresses in locations which were advantageous for communication. When the period of conquest was over, many of these fortresses were turned into towns. The population grew, and architectural works, such as forums and marketplaces, were introduced. Almost all of the Britannic towns attained the status of civitas. Their economic foundations were mainly agricultural. Londinium was an exception to the rule and attained great urban development based on its river port and on the network of roads which converged there. It enjoyed great economic prosperity until the end of the second century.

Society and Economy

Only a few Romans settled in the new province, and the majority of the population continued to be Celtic. The society which developed was composed of families which were

TERRITORY OF THE GERMANS

Rhine

Noviomagus

Colonia Traiana

Novaesium

GERMANIA INFERIOR

Colonia Agrippinensis

Bonna

Meuse

Mosel

Mogontiacum

GERMANIA SUPERIOR

Augusta Treverorum

Argentoratum

Danube

Regina Castra

BELGICA (GAUL)

RHAETIA

Augusta Vindelicum

On the map are provinces along the Gallic-Germanic border.

People are shown in front of the gateway of the Augustian colony of Treverorum, today called Trier. In the first century A.D., it was the seat of the official responsible for the provinces of Belgica Gaul and the two German provinces. The men and woman on the chariot are wearing the typical clothing of the empire.

The artisan quarter of a German town on the Rhine is seen.

wealthy enough to aspire to senatorial positions, of knights, and of rich common people. The counselors who were in charge of the magistratures of the towns were taken from the above groups. Merchants, artisans, and slaves also lived in the towns. Roman customs and behavior spread among the inhabitants of Britannia, both to the aristocracy and commoners. The first and foremost custom was the use of the toga. The Latin language became the language of government and of culture, while the traditional Celtic language was used in family life. The number of villas rapidly multiplied in the rural areas just outside the urban centers. The

wealth of Britannia was connected to the extraction of coal and metals such as lead, gold, and iron.

Rome and the Germans

Beginning at the end of the first century B.C., the presence of Germanic populations increased on the Celtic side of the Rhine. This was due to the Roman policy of giving tracts of land to farmers, provided they would settle there. This policy caused a great mingling of populations in the regions near the borders. The German tribes had a political organization similar to the Celtic tribes and were deeply influenced by the

Celts along the Rhine. The custom of serving in the auxiliary troops of the Roman army had put them in contact with elements of Roman civilization. As a result, not all of the Germans were absolutely opposed to the way of life of the conquerors. However, due to their military strength, the Germans were greatly feared by the Celts and Romans. Thus, the relationship between the Germans and the Romans alternated between caution and sudden assaults, followed by treaties, commercial relationships, the exchange of goods, and movements of populations.

The Two Germanys
—Borderlands

The German territories of the Roman empire, divided into Germania Superior and Germania Inferior, stretched along the Rhine and included lands which are today part of Germany, Holland, Belgium, and France. Due to the location of this territory along the border of the empire, the presence of a military contingency was considerable at over 100,000 men. The process of Romanization occurred according to political and military requirements.

THE ROMAN EMPIRE AND THE POPULATION OF THE BALKANS

During the rule of Augustus, the provinces south of the Danube had also been conquered by the Roman Empire. These areas were inhabited by various populations. Noricum, Pannonia, and the internal areas of the Moesia were inhabited by Celts. The Illyrian populations prevailed in the rest of the region.

The Illyrian Lands

The annexation of the Illyrians to the Roman Empire opened a new chapter in their history, bringing forth important changes in all areas of material and spiritual life. The Romans further developed the towns which existed along the Adriatic coast. In the countryside and in the rugged mountains, Roman penetration was slower, particularly in the first centuries of Roman domination.

Pannonia

The Romans found the Celts had highly developed agricultural techniques in Pannonia, the vast plain which is today part of Hungary and which stretches all the way to the Danube. The arrival of the Romans caused the development of a wealthy, highly civilized Celtic-Roman world.

The Dacian Wars

The Dacians were a people living along the two banks of the lower reaches of the Danube, between the Black Sea and the Carpathian Mountains. They were descendants of ancient Thracians, but their culture had been influenced by neighboring steppe peoples. Greece had also influenced the Dacians. These populations took on Roman elements, mainly in their economy, defense, and culture. They were an independent people, highly skilled in warfare. They had already made numerous excursions against the Celts of Pannonia and of areas north of the Danube. When the Romans settled along the Danube, Dacian bands frequently raided and looted the Roman provinces. In A.D. 101, Trajan (who had just been elected emperor) decided to pursue war. The Dacians had learned the fighting techniques of the Romans and had a large army in battle, each soldier armed with the fearsome battle scimitar. The allies of the Dacians, the Rhoxolani, were nomadic tribes living along the northern coast of the Black Sea who possessed an armored cavalry furnished with a full array of weapons. A chain of fortresses surrounded the Dacian capital, Sarmizegethusa. The Romans embarked on the war with great zeal, but the conquest of the Dacia required two vigorous campaigns which were carried out without mercy and the sparing of human life. The war was finally concluded with the victorious entrance of Trajan into the Dacian capital, the suicide of the Dacian king, and the deportation of the defeated peoples.

The Romanization of the Dacian Lands

In the lands of conquered Dacia, the process of Romanization was mainly carried out through the settlement of Roman people. Colonies and municipalities were founded and multiplied near military campgrounds. Most likely, the Dacian populations were not completely eliminated by war and deportation.

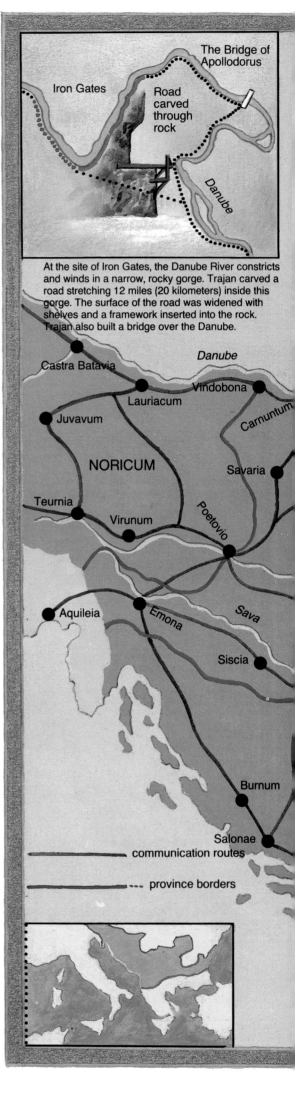

At the site of Iron Gates, the Danube River constricts and winds in a narrow, rocky gorge. Trajan carved a road stretching 12 miles (20 kilometers) inside this gorge. The surface of the road was widened with shelves and a framework inserted into the rock. Trajan also built a bridge over the Danube.

communication routes

--- province borders

The Balkan-Danubian region between the Adriatic and Black seas is shown.

Pictured is a cavalryman of the Rhoxolani, the allies of the Dacians against the Romans.

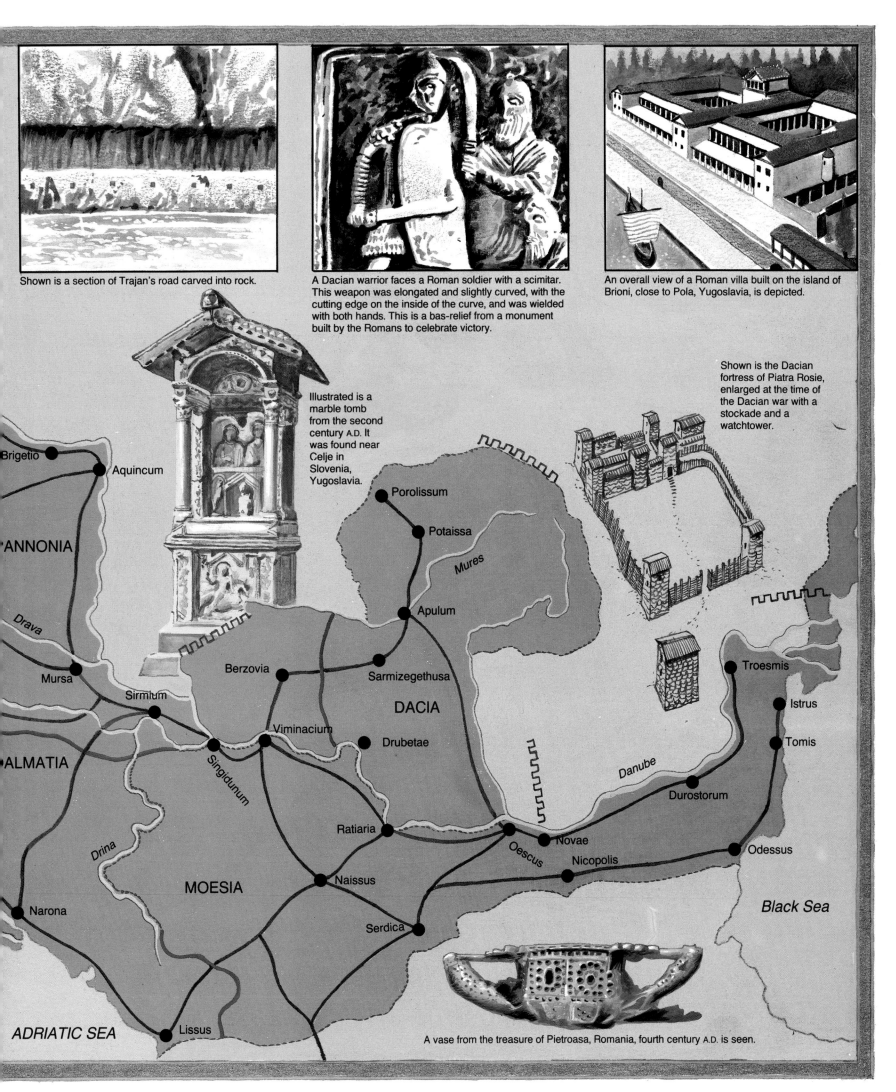

Shown is a section of Trajan's road carved into rock.

A Dacian warrior faces a Roman soldier with a scimitar. This weapon was elongated and slightly curved, with the cutting edge on the inside of the curve, and was wielded with both hands. This is a bas-relief from a monument built by the Romans to celebrate victory.

An overall view of a Roman villa built on the island of Brioni, close to Pola, Yugoslavia, is depicted.

Illustrated is a marble tomb from the second century A.D. It was found near Celje in Slovenia, Yugoslavia.

Shown is the Dacian fortress of Piatra Rosie, enlarged at the time of the Dacian war with a stockade and a watchtower.

Brigetio

Aquincum

PANNONIA

Drava

Mursa

Sirmium

DALMATIA

Narona

Porolissum

Potaissa

Mures

Apulum

Berzovia

Sarmizegethusa

DACIA

Viminacium

Drubetae

Singidunum

Troesmis

Istrus

Tomis

Danube

Durostorum

Drina

Ratiaria

Oescus

Novae

Nicopolis

Odessus

Naissus

MOESIA

Black Sea

Serdica

ADRIATIC SEA

Lissus

A vase from the treasure of Pietroasa, Romania, fourth century A.D. is seen.

THE EASTERN PROVINCES

Rome and the Hellenistic World

After the death of Alexander the Great, a flourishing civilization of Greek origin, but heavily influenced by eastern civilizations, developed in the coastal towns of Asia Minor. It was called Hellenism. The Romans had always feared the commercial proficiency of the Greek world and were in deep awe of its cultural superiority. They defended the Greeks and subsequently dominated them, but were also disciples eager to learn the Greek culture and bring it to the west. Beginning with the last century of the Republican Age, the Romans brought to their capital, from Greece, works of art and literature which were kept in the Roman domus and in the cities. With the advent of the Imperial Age, the unity of the Roman world became the main way of spreading Hellenistic culture. The blend of Hellenistic and Roman cultures was productive and allowed the empire to continue ruling the eastern lands for over one thousand years.

The Provinces of Asia and the East

In the Macedonian towns in the regions of Lycia and Pamphylia and in Asia, Roman dominion allowed for the enrichment of urban life and favored the spread of Hellenism to the interior regions. These towns had important strategic locations because they were crossed by a major communication route between the Mediterranean and the Indian Ocean. More to the east, the Cappadocia region and the kingdom of Armenia were geographically isolated from the major commercial routes and centers of culture. However, they slowly absorbed several Hellenistic influences for the Greek language was spoken at the court of the Armenian king, and many Greeks lived in the country. The Romans conquered Cappadocia first, then Armenia. Armenia was a defense against the Parthian kingdom, great enemies of the empire. As a consequence, numerous military posts were established in these regions, and a network

Pictured is Ephesus, the capital of the Roman province in Asia, as reconstructed according to archaeological excavations. The frieze with ships on top of the page is a reproduction of a bas-relief found in Ostia, Italy.

Center map: Provinces of Asia Minor and the Middle East are shown.

of roads was built to ship supplies. Moreover, major strategic roads were built to connect this land with the Aegean Sea and to facilitate communication with the posts along the Danube. Consequently, the commercial activities in Armenia and Cappadocia greatly increased. Russian wheat, for example, passed through these regions on its way to the military posts along the Euphrates. This borderline with the Parthians represented the maximum point of expansion of Roman rule in the east.

The Middle Eastern Provinces

The circumstances of the middle eastern provinces were in sharp contrast to the ones in the west. These provinces were Judaea, Syria, Mesopotamia, and Assyria. These regions were crossed by major rivers and were rich in fertile plains. They were the center of a very active commerce. Syria in particular, due to its position on the Mediterranean, had always been the starting point of important land communication routes directed toward the Persian Gulf and India. Upon the arrival of the Romans, a flourishing Hellenistic civilization already existed in most of these regions and the towns were highly developed. Rome built new provinces on top of that which already existed and sent its officers only to the areas which had solid local government. Public works, such as the construction of aqueducts and new irrigation channels, expanded farming to less fertile areas. The production of wheat and grains became outstanding. Wine from Syria was imported both by the east and the west. Olive groves provided plentiful oil, while vast fruit groves replenished the markets of the empire. Other characteristic Syrian activities were weaving, glassmaking, and the production of a rare purple dye from sea snails. The camel began to be used as an animal of transport, and long caravans of these beasts would leave the city markets of the coast and cross the interior areas, following routes which would pass towns, oases, and water wells. The diversity of contacts and the mingling of populations also favored the spread of different religions. The traditional Greek religion and several eastern cults coexisted in these provinces of the empire. They found receptive audiences in the mixed populations of the port and caravan towns, as well as in the army campgrounds.

Depicted is a marketplace of a town placed along one of the caravan routes of the interior. The Middle East drew its wealth from trade between the Mediterranean and the Orient. The frieze with the camel caravan shown on the top of the page was found in the caravan town of Palmyra.

CRISIS IN ROMAN RELIGION

The religious practices performed by the emperor with great pomp could not meet all the religious needs of a diverse empire.

The Roman Army and the Spread of the Mystery Cults

People were still looking for a solution to their sense of anxiety about life and the uncertainty of the future. The fear of a possible fall of Rome could be compared to a nightmarish idea of the end of the world. An increasing number of people began joining eastern cults, also called mystery cults. Most of the religious activities of these cults were kept secret from outsiders. Besides the Egyptian cult of Isis, there were the cults of Cybele from Asia Minor, Baal (the warrior god), and Sol Indictus (a sun-god of Syrian origin). Within the Roman Empire, there were some restrictions about joining cults. The major concern of the Romans was that the cult of the emperor not be threatened. The Roman army encountered local cults in the various eastern provinces where it settled. Later, these cults were introduced by the army to Rome and throughout the empire. The new religions seemed to give an answer to the spiritual crises of the people, who in the meantime could continue to partake in the public events of the imperial cult.

The faithful could have a personal religious experience which gave them a renewed spiritual peace and a renewed enthusiasm. Processions of the various eastern cults were emotionally moving experiences, greatly different from the Roman liturgical formalities.

Stoicism

The same sense of discontent over Roman religion was also felt by cultured people like the great noble Roman families and even the imperial family. In fact, Roman religion was reduced to public shows and devoid of any spiritual interest for the people. The way was open for a philosophy called "stoicism" which had started some centuries earlier in Athens through the works of Zeno. Wisdom was considered to be the ability to recognize the existence of order in the world. Men of reason had to accept what happened to them and could not give in to emotions. On the one hand, this philosophy was pessimistic about the possibilities of changing the circumstances of one's own life or that of other people. On the other hand, it encouraged moderation, a moral effort to lead a virtuous life, and human solidarity and respect for everyone. This philosophy was, however, known only among the cultured people and the upper class.

A legionnaire is shown during movement of troops. The army was a major means for the transfer of different religions as it carried beliefs and cults from one end of the empire to the other, even introducing them to highly civilized populations.

1) Shown is part of a bronze, triangular votive table depicting Baal, the powerful Hittite god of war, being worshipped by soldiers of the empire. He stands on the sacred bull, and above him there is a bust of the sun—Germany, third century A.D. **2)** A priest of Cybele is dressed in Oriental fashion holding in his right hand three sprigs of wheat, the symbol of fertility. **3)** A procession in honor of Isis is held.

In the house of a great Roman family, a group of Christians has gathered for a baptism. The new convert will thus become fully part of the Christian community.

CHRISTIANITY

In this climate, tense but also rich in new ideas and spiritual reawakening, a new event that was destined to have an impact without precedent in human history was on the verge of taking place. In Palestine, during the empire of Trajan, a man was crucified because he was judged guilty of offending the Hebrew religion. The Roman governor, Pilate, allowed the execution. This man, Jesus of Nazareth, allegedly proclaimed himself son of God, the Messiah of whom the Hebrew scriptures spoke. The writings of the disciples of Jesus, called the Gospel,

gave an account of the life and message which Jesus left to humanity. Jesus, also called Christ (or Messiah, which means the consecrated king), brought testimony to the world that God was not an incomprehensible power but was father of all. Christianity was the proclamation of the friendship between God and people. Christ was said to have risen from the dead. He became a major figure in history. For most Hebrews, this was a scandal. They expected a magnificent king and not a common man born in the small village of Bethlehem. To the Greco-

Roman world, Christ seemed a ludicrous figure, a god who had become a man in order to accompany humankind on earth and on to eternity, a god who went as far as being crucified to remove the sins of humanity, a god who told people that if they accepted him he would always be with them. Although all of this seemed ridiculous to most Romans, the number of people who believed in the new religion grew slowly but steadily. Christianity spread from Palestine to the rest of the empire, especially in the eastern provinces, in the army, among the common people, and also in the great Roman families. Life as a Christian did not mean the observance of a series of regulations, but it required new, major responsibilities. It called for a new way to perform daily activities because the meaning of life could be found in the smallest detail. Everything could be considered a gesture of love, toward Christ and toward people.

Christians and the Empire

Christians did not deny the sovereignty of the emperor and preached obedience to the law. For this reason, in the beginning, the imperial authorities had no reason to hinder the practice of Christianity. Also, the Christians were often helpful in the service of the empire. The imperial administration, however, could not accept the fact that Christians would not worship the emperor as a god. This was considered a disruption of the Pax Deorum. The cause for the persecutions was not a fear of political turmoil but the fear of offending the gods and thereby shaking the solidity of the Roman Empire. The persecutions were periods in which the Christians were imprisoned, tortured, and put to violent death. Even members of the imperial families were sometimes persecuted. Periods of persecutions alternated with periods of peaceful coexistence. The first persecution was carried out in A.D. 64 by Nero. The second was ordered by Domitian. The rule of the Antonine emperors (especially Hadrian and the Antoninus Pius) was a happy period during which Christians began to have an influence on Roman culture. Philip the Arab was the first Christian emperor, followed by Decius and Valerian, who resumed the persecutions. The last major persecution was ordered by Diocletian. Christianity questioned the value of the divinity of the emperor, and in so doing opposed a basic point of the Roman order. On the other hand, it was in agreement with a more important element of Roman civilization—the desire for an alliance with the divine.

THE GERMANS AGAINST THE EMPIRE

Social Ranking

At the end of the first century A.D. when the Roman, Tacitus, wrote an important essay on Germany, important changes had occurred in the part of the German world closest to the empire. These were the result of contact with the Romans, especially with merchants who traveled through German lands. Luxury goods and Mediterranean wealth circulated among the most powerful men of the tribes, and some forms of social ranking developed.

The Marcomanni and Quadi North of the Danube

Since the first century A.D., Marcomanni and Quadi had settled north of the Danube in today's Czechoslovakia. Being close to the border, they had numerous commercial and cultural contacts with the Roman Empire. They developed an agricultural economy which required the possession of wider territories. Gradually, the various tribal groups started to recognize that they had interests and aims in common.

The Roman Limes Collapse

The Romans living along the Danube were not especially good at understanding or taking advantage of the changes that were happening on the other side of the river. The Germans had never been granted any settlement in Roman territory, and they could not navigate the Danube. Moreover, on their side of the river, Romans established a security zone where no barbarians could settle. Around the middle of the second century, barbarians threatened the middle reaches of the Danube. As soon as Rome sent troops to fight the Parthians from this border, Germans invaded the empire. In 167, Marcomanni, Quadi, and twenty other German tribes under the guidance of King Bellovesus attacked a long stretch of the Danube. The Roman troops, weakened by a serious wave of plague, did not successfully resist. The Germans, after devastating Pannonia, reached Italy. They arrived in Venetum and laid siege to Aquileia.

The Victorious Reaction of the Romans

It was a difficult time for Rome. Many soldiers and officers were dead, and the empire had inadequate financial resources. The emperor Marcus Aurelius assumed personal leadership of the army. The Germans were forced to abandon Italy in 172, and the Roman legions counterattacked.

At right: In A.D. 170, German tribes made the first raid on Italy, breaking through from the Tarvisio or from the Slovenian Alps.

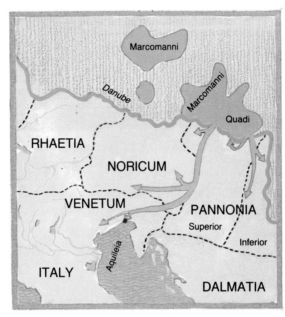

The invasions of Marcomanni and Quadi into the empire are shown.

The Plan of Marcus Aurelius

Marcus Aurelius hoped victory would allow the further expansion of the empire. He planned to create two provinces past the Danube, Marcomannia and Sarmatia. The new border was to fall on the northern mountains, which were easy to defend. Marcus Aurelius died in Vienna in 180 and was succeeded by his son, Commodus, who did not carry out his father's plan.

At right: During the last phase of the war, the Roman army crossed the Danube and for a short time established an advanced contingent north of the river.

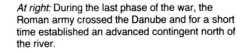

Shown are two iron lance points used by the Germans with magical signs engraved in silver.

Above are Roman soldiers with prisoners and cattle, the loot of war. This image is from the Column of Antoninus.

Diocletian ordered that a great palace be built for him in Spalatum on the Yugoslavian coast. The palace was composed of several buildings surrounded by a fortified enclosure. The complex had a rectangular shape and stretched over 660 feet (200 meters). In building his palace, Diocletian blended styles and details from throughout the empire.

THE GREAT CRISIS OF THE EMPIRE AND DIOCLETIAN

The Third Century, A Period of Crisis

The death of Commodus in 192 opened a dramatic period in Roman history. The Romans lived with fears concerning the future, and a sense of the imminent fall of the empire was in the air. The ancient Etruscan prophecies about the rise and fall of civilizations in history seemed on the verge of coming true for Rome. Famine and pestilence caused a major crisis in some provinces such as Britannia. Robberies by an undisciplined army and barbarian raids markedly weakened the countryside, affecting even wealthy people. Due to great danger in some areas, villas were abandoned and all agricultural activities stopped. The economic crisis was followed by a monetary crisis, mostly due to the great expense of maintaining the army. Taxes were heavy, but never sufficient. The emperors started minting copper coins instead of silver ones, and the currency soon devaluated causing steep price increases.

From Septimius Severus to Caracalla

In 193, troops from the provinces marched on Rome, guided by the African Lucius Septimius Severus. He was the commander of the Pannonian army and became emperor after defeating three rivals. Upon his death, his son Caracalla ascended the throne. In 212, Caracalla issued a constitution which granted Roman citizenship to all the free inhabitants of the empire. This completed a process of Romanization which had lasted for centuries but was also a sign that the Roman Empire was changing. All of the citizens were equal, but they were ruled by a despotic and absolute sovereign, more similar to eastern kings than to earlier Roman rulers.

Pressure from the Barbarians Increases

Taking advantage of the internal turmoil, the enemy broke through the border from several points and swarmed into the empire. German tribes formed an alliance and made plans to conquer the European provinces. Franks and Alemanni threatened Gaul, Saxons looted Britannia and Gaul, and Marcomanni pushed on the Danube.

The Army Elects the Emperors

The death of Alexander Severus in 235 extinguished the house of the Severi, and the empire fell under the control of the army. Between 235 and 285, twenty-six emperors elected by various military detachments alternated in ruling the empire. No strong authority existed, and devastation swept the provinces.

Inserts (at top of page) show some aspects of the crisis of the third century. From left to right: Political instability and the frequent assassination of the emperors; pressure from the barbarians; looting and devastation carried out by rebellious troops; and the desertion of the villas, which had become very dangerous places live.

Diocletian Created the Tetrarchy

In 284, the Roman army proclaimed the Illyric high officer Valerius Aurelius Diocletian emperor. The people were tired and disgusted. They longed for peace and were willing to collaborate in a reform policy. Diocletian introduced the system of the tetrarchy (a government ruled by four people).

He divided the territory of the empire in half, each of which was ruled by two men—an Augustus on top and and a Caesar. Diocletian was the Augustus of the eastern provinces and resided in Nicomedia in Asia Minor. His Caesar lived in Sirmium on the Balkans. The Augustus of the western provinces was Massiminus, who resided in Milanum. His Caesar lived in Trier. The tetrarchy was also meant to solve the problem of imperial succession because each Caesar was to eventually become Augustus without previous approval by the senate or acclamation by the legions. Diocletian himself started the succession process, abdicat-ing in 305 and retiring into his palace in Spalatum on the Dalmatian coast.

The Administrative System and the Reform of the Army

The power of the emperor was absolute, and his will was enacted by a tight network of officials. This system caused the collapse of the ancient nobility and of the traditional Roman magistratures. The imperial administration ruled with military discipline, and as a result the unity of the empire was strengthened. Huge masses of soldiers were drafted even among the less Romanized populations. The army was composed of as many as 350,000 soldiers. In the face of massive recruitment, the ancient provincial armies lost much of their importance. They were composed of colonists who had hereditary duty to serve in the army. Major changes accompanied the reformation of the army, and the main towns of the empire were gradually surrounded by fortified walls.

The Persecution of Christians

In order to sustain his power, Diocletian proclaimed himself to be the ruler sent by Jupiter and affirmed that his power had a divine origin. Therefore, he revived the practice of the imperial cult. In 303, he launched into the last violent and major persecution against the Christians, who had become numerous throughout the empire with converts among the military and civilians.

A Christian has been arrested by soldiers.

Constantine is acclaimed Augustus by his legionnaires in York, England, in A.D. 306.

Right: In Italy in 311, Constantine fought for dominion of the empire against the other Augustus, Maxentius. The two armies clashed in Rome, on the Tiber, close to the Mulvian Bridge. On top of a temporary pontoon bridge, the troops of Maxentium were defeated by those of Constantine who had put a Christian symbol on each of their shields.

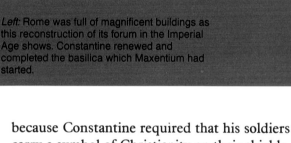

Left: Rome was full of magnificent buildings as this reconstruction of its forum in the Imperial Age shows. Constantine renewed and completed the basilica which Maxentium had started.

FROM ROME TO BYZANTIUM

The Failure of the Tetrarchy

The solution to the problem of the central authority devised by Diocletian did not last long. After abdicating, Diocletian helplessly witnessed internal struggles between Augustii and Caesarii for the division of power. After several years of harsh struggle, Constantine, a man native to Illyria, finally triumphed.

The Rise of Constantine

Constantine was proclaimed Augustus by his legions in York, Britannia, in 306. In 311, he entered Rome and fought for power against his rival Maxentius, the other Augustus who had been elected in Rome. The following year, he finally defeated Maxentius in the battle of the Mulvian Bridge. This event has become famous because Constantine required that his soldiers carry a symbol of Christianity on their shields. He followed instructions received in a dream in which he was promised victory. In 324, Constantine defeated his last rival, Licinius, in the eastern provinces and became the sole ruler of the empire.

Constantine and Christianity

Most Christians had survived Diocletian's persecution, and both the distribution and the strength of their faith became increasingly evident. The Church was becoming a major force, capable of exerting a lasting influence on society. In 313 in Milanum, Constantine issued an edict in which he conceded freedom of practice for all religions.

The Second Rome

The eastern provinces became the most important part of the empire. Their economy, based on sea traffic and on caravan routes, was still flourishing. Moreover, the borders which most needed to be patrolled were in the eastern areas and in the Balkan province. Thus, the center of the empire needed to be shifted, both for economic and for strategic reasons. But another reason also prompted Constantine to abandon Rome. The city was still the pagan center, while the eastern provinces were becoming the most vital centers of Christianity. Constantine decided upon the founding of a new city on the Bosporus Strait where the sea lanes of the Aegean Sea and the Black Sea met. The new city, capital of the empire, was Byzantium, later called Constantinople. It was meant to imitate Rome in grandeur and in the abun-

Wishing to give a Christian mark to the empire, Constantine built a new capital in the east called Constantinople. It was splendid and full of churches where only the new Christian God was worshipped in public. Shown is the emperor arriving by boat in A.D. 330 to inaugurate the new city.

Among the counselors and friends of Constantine was Bishop Eusebius of Caesarea, who advised him on several issues of ecclesiastic policy. In the picture, the bishop is explaining some notions of the Christian doctrine to the emperor *(left)*.

dance of public buildings and monuments, but it would not have public sites for pagan cults. It was to be a Christian city. The city plan was carefully drawn, and construction proceeded rapidly. Works of art from all of the Hellenistic Orient were collected into the city, and the best craftspeople were employed. On May 11, in 330, Constantine solemnly inaugurated the new city, the second Rome.

The Christian Roman Empire

It was the completion of the major transformation which had begun over fifty years earlier. The Roman Empire as it had been during Augustus no longer existed. It had been replaced by a different political system. No one doubted the divine origin of the emperor. He was attributed divine characteristics and was considered the vicar of god on earth. A highly solemn ritual, derived from Persian traditions, was used to insure that everyone paid elaborate homage to the imperial majesty. The emperor had unlimited authority, and a huge number of officials at his service executed his will, even at the most remote towns.

The Decline of Rome

Rome and its empire (which was later to be called the Western Empire) were in increasing danger. War and invasions hung over a world which was doomed to disintegrate but which would also leave great contributions to civilizations yet to come. Byzantium was the city which preserved the tradition of Rome at its best, together with Christianity, which had given a new sense to human life and destiny. From Byzantium, the most important features of clas-sical Roman civilization were to be passed on to Europe: the alliance between God and humans and the legal system as a guarantee for civil coexistence. It was the end of the ancient world, and a new page was opening in the history of Europe and the Middle East.

A Roman bowman serving in a division of the auxiliary troops of the eastern provinces is pictured.

69

Caledonia

Antonine's Wall

Hadrian's Wall

York

BRITANNIA

London

Rhine

GERMANIA

Colonia

Mainz

Treviri

Paris

Strasbourg

Alesia

GAUL

Bordeaux

ATLANTIC OCEAN

Danube

RAETIA

NORICUM

Vienna

Budapest

Celje

Aquileia

PANNONIA

Sarmizegethusa

DACIA

Milan

Pola

Sirmium

Danube

Zara

Spalatum

DALMATIA

Nis

MOESIA

Aix

Marseille

ITALY

Numantia

THRACE

HISPANIA

MACEDONIA

Saguntum

Rome

Gades

ACHAIA

Athens

Tangier

Agrigentum

Syracuse

Sparta

Cirta

Carthage

MAURETANIA

AFRICA PROCONSOLARIA

Mediterranean Sea

Cyrene

Sabrata

Leptis Magne

CYRENAICA

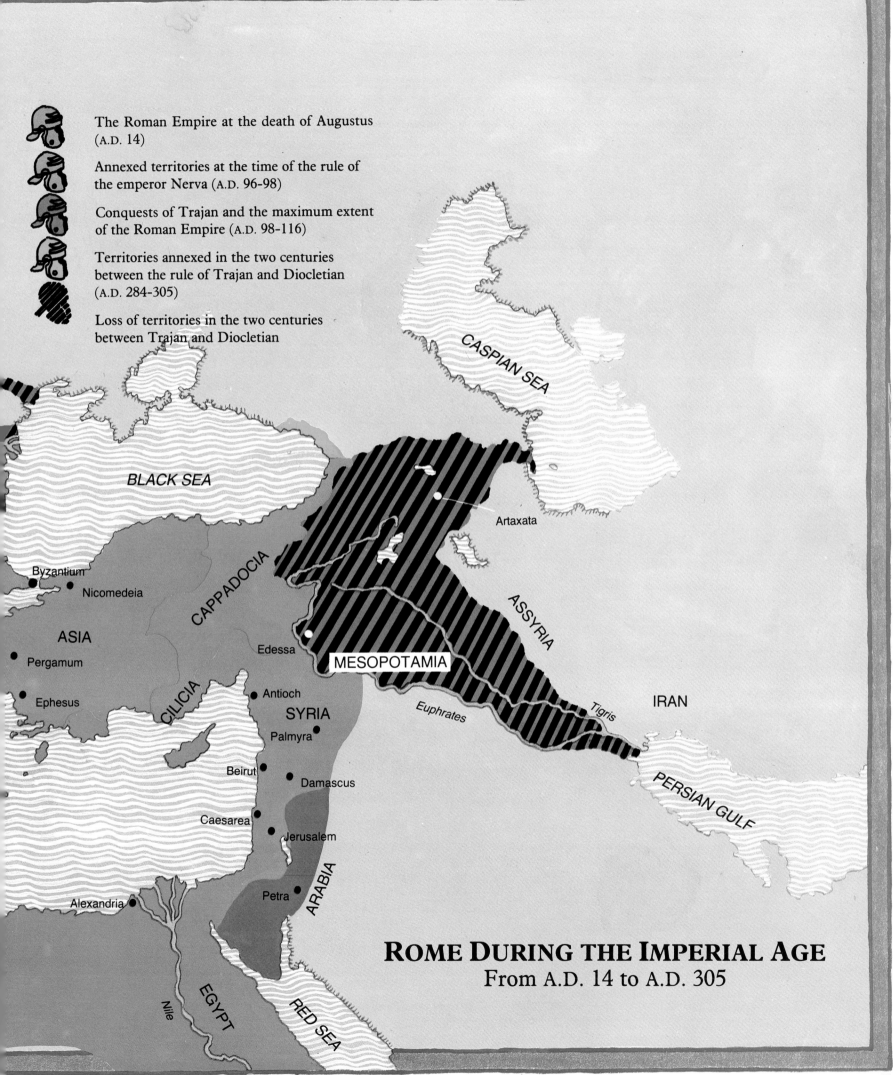

The Roman Empire at the death of Augustus
(A.D. 14)

Annexed territories at the time of the rule of
the emperor Nerva (A.D. 96-98)

Conquests of Trajan and the maximum extent
of the Roman Empire (A.D. 98-116)

Territories annexed in the two centuries
between the rule of Trajan and Diocletian
(A.D. 284-305)

Loss of territories in the two centuries
between Trajan and Diocletian

CASPIAN SEA

BLACK SEA

Artaxata

Byzantium

Nicomedeia

CAPPADOCIA

ASSYRIA

ASIA

Pergamum

Edessa

MESOPOTAMIA

Ephesus

CILICIA

IRAN

Antioch

Euphrates

Tigris

SYRIA

Palmyra

Beirut

Damascus

PERSIAN GULF

Caesarea

Jerusalem

ARABIA

Alexandria

Petra

ROME DURING THE IMPERIAL AGE
From A.D. 14 to A.D. 305

Nile

EGYPT

RED SEA

GLOSSARY

aggressive: ready and willing to fight or take action; eager to participate fully.

agora: a meeting place or assembly area.

agriculture: the processes and activities associated with farming; the work of planting seeds, producing crops, and raising animals.

aqueduct: a pipe system used to transport water from a distant place.

archaic: of or belonging to ancient times.

artisan: a skilled craftsperson.

autonomous: capable of existing alone and apart from others.

barbarian: a member of a primitive or uncivilized tribe or group; a savage.

ceramics: objects made of clay that are molded into shape and baked in an oven.

chivalry: the noble qualities of knighthood, dating back to medieval times. Chivalrous qualities included courage, honesty, and gallantry.

cuirass: a leather breastplate, used as armor by the ancient Greek warriors.

cult: a specific or distinct type of religious worship or ritual. Greek religion is usually identified with the cult of the gods of Mount Olympus.

cultivate: to prepare land for the planting and growing of crops.

culture: the traditions, skills, habits, and systems of different groups of people at different times in history.

currency: the medium of exchange, or money used, in any country or region.

deity: a god; a being who possesses a divine nature.

demiurge: a magistrate or other person given the power to administer the law.

democracy: a government which is in the hands of the people.

dialogue: a conversation between two or more people. Plato used dialogue as a method of teaching and learning.

duel: a fight between two people, usually witnessed by others for the purpose of fairness.

dynasty: a family of rulers; the period of time during which a specific family is in power.

environment: the circumstances or conditions of a plant or animal's surroundings. The physical and social conditions of an organism's environment influence its growth and development.

expedition: a journey or exploratory mission undertaken in order to achieve a specific purpose.

fraternity: brotherhood; a group of people joined together by common interest or purpose.

frieze: a series of decorations positioned to form a border around a room or building.

gladiator: a man who fought with weapons against other men or animals in an arena or coliseum in ancient Rome. Gladiators fought as a form of entertainment for nobility and the public.

heritage: cultural characteristics that are handed down or passed on from one generation to the next.

ingot: a piece of metal, formed into the shape of a bar, used as currency in ancient times.

lance: a spearlike weapon.

lottery: a game based on luck or chance, in which people buy numbered tickets in the hope of winning prizes or money.

magistrate: a government official who is granted the powers to effect justice.

maritime: having to do with the sea or with the shipping industry.

melancholy: the condition of being sad, gloomy, or depressed.

mercenary: hired soldiers; soldiers paid to fight battles in foreign countries.

migrate: to move from place to place in search of food and shelter. Migration usually revolves around seasonal changes.

minority: a small portion of an otherwise large group; less than half of the whole.

mint: to make money or other currency which is authorized by the government.

monarch: the primary ruler of a state or kingdom, such as a king or queen.

monologue: a long speech delivered by one person. Ancient Greek actors often delivered monologues.

oligarchy: a government run by a few select people. Noblemen formed oligarchies in ancient Greece.

oracle: any person who is believed to be capable of communication with the gods.

orator: a person who is skilled at delivering speeches in public. The Greek Pericles was an excellent orator.

patrician: in the society of ancient Rome, a member of a noble or prominent family. Most political positions of that time were held by patricians.

peninsula: a land area almost entirely surrounded by water and connected to the mainland by a narrow strip of earth called an isthmus.

pessimism: the attitude toward life that the worst will always happen; the belief that more bad than good exists in the world.

plebeian: in the society of ancient Rome, one of the common people or the lower classes.

polis: a city-state in ancient Greece. Involvement in the business of the polis meant involvement in politics.

prehistoric: referring to a period of time before recorded history.

primitive: of or existing in the beginning or the earliest times; ancient.

produce: fresh fruit and vegetables.

prologue: an introduction; the first part or portion of a literary work used as preparation for what follows.

retreat: to move away from a place of danger toward a place of safety.

revenue: income; the money which a business or government is able to generate for itself through taxation, profit, and other sources.

ritual: a system of acts or procedures, especially with regard to religious worship.

sanctuary: a place of peace or safety; a haven or place of rest; a special building set aside for holy worship.

siren: in Greek mythology, one of several beautiful women who lured sailors to their deaths along rocky coastlines. The sailors could not resist the haunting songs of the sirens.

sovereign: a supreme ruler; one who possesses authority above all others.

tragedy: a type of play invented by the Greeks that always ends sadly or disastrously.

tyrant: a supreme ruler, usually one who does not tolerate the wishes or opinions of his subjects.

valley: a stretch of low land that lies between hills or mountains and usually has a stream or river flowing through it.

vineyard: an area of land used to grow grapes, usually for the purpose of making wine.

INDEX

A

Acropolis, 16-17
Actium, battle of, 41
Aeschylus, 25
agora, 7
Alexander the Great, 20, 27, 28-29, 60
alphabet, 10
Antigone, , 24
Antony, Mark, 42
aqueducts, 61
Aquileia, 64
Archaic Age, 7, 10, 20
architecture, Greek, 21
Ariovistus, 39
Aristophanes, 25
Aristotle, 27
Armenia, 60-61
arminius, 43
army, Roman, 52, 53, 62
art, Greek, 6, 20-21
artisans, Celtic, 37
assembly, 11
Assyria, 61
Athens, 12, 13, 14, 15, 16, 20, 27, 28
athletics, 23
atomistic school, 26
Attica, 12
Augustus, 45, 46, 50, 51, 52, 58, 69
Aurelius, Marcus, 64

B

barbarians, 66
Bellovesus, 64
Britannia, 56, 66, 68
Byzantium, 68-69

C

Caesar, Julius, 37, 39, 41
camel, 61
Cappadocia, 60-61
Caracalla, 66
Carthage, 19
Carthaginians, 8, 34-35
cavalry, 12
Celtic (language), 57
Celts, 36, 37, 38-39, 56, 58
Christ, 63

Christian, 67
Christianity, 63
Cicero, 41, 50
citizen, 14
city-state, 6, 7
civitas, 53
Classical Age, 7, 20
Cleisthenes, 13
Cleopatra, 42
clients, 33
coins, 10, 15, 28, 40
colonization
    Greek, 8-9, 18
    Roman, 52, 58
comedy, 24, 25
comitia, 35
Comitia Centuriata, 32
Comitia Curiata, 32
Comitia Tributa, 32
Commodus, 64, 66
Constantine, 68, 69
construction, 21
Corinthian order, 21
council, 11
cult of the dead, 22
cults, 62
culture, Spain, 54
currency, 10, 15
customs, Roman, 57
Cybele, 62
Cyme, 18

D

Dacians, 58
Darius, 14
Dark Ages, 6
democracy, 14
Democritos, 26-27
Diacria, 13
Diocletian, Valerius Aurelius, 67, 68
Dionysus, 24
Dominatus, 31
Domitian, 63
domus, 48, 60
Dorian order, 20
Dorians, 13
Doric order, 21

tragedy, 24-25
Trajan, 52, 54, 58, 63
tyranny, 18
tyrant, 11, 12

U, V, X, Z